AND INDUSTRIAL RELATIONS
IN *SPAIN*

D1369173

THE TRADE UNION SITUATION AND INDUSTRIAL RELATIONS IN *SPAIN*

REPORT OF AN ILO MISSION

INTERNATIONAL LABOUR OFFICE   GENEVA

U41207 c

ISBN 92-2-105202-8

First published 1985

Printed in Switzerland   ATA

In 1984 the ILO published the first two in a series of studies on the trade union situation and industrial relations in various economic and social systems in Europe. Hungary and Norway were the first two countries to be studied. At its 229th Session in February-March 1985, the Governing Body of the International Labour Office decided to publish two further studies, this time concerned with Spain and Yugoslavia. The present publication contains the report on Spain, the report on Yugoslavia being published separately.

These studies have been undertaken by the Office in accordance with resolutions adopted in 1974 and 1979 by the Second and Third European Regional Conferences. The Conference had noted that not enough was known about industrial relations structures and systems in Europe. It had expressed the wish that these questions should be analysed in the most exhaustive manner possible, in the light of the international labour standards adopted by the ILO, as well as of the experience acquired and data collected by the competent ILO supervisory bodies.

It need hardly be said that these studies are in no way to be regarded as a substitute for the procedures of supervision of the application of international labour Conventions. Indeed, they are very different both in their nature and in their objectives. The procedures of supervision are basically aimed at allowing problems to be examined at the general level of principles and juridical obligations, within the framework of the constitutional provisions of the Organisation which are binding on member States. Furthermore, when complaints procedures in particular are involved, the supervisory bodies examine only the specific questions with which they are concerned, without conducting a general survey of the trade union situation in the country involved.

The studies, on the other hand, were carried out in a climate far removed from any conflict on the application of a particular international labour standard, and the countries concerned agreed to them on a voluntary basis.

The Governments of Spain and Yugoslavia, like those of Hungary and Norway before them, invited the International Labour Office to send missions to their respective countries. A team of ILO officials therefore undertook an in-depth analysis of the legislation and of the current industrial relations situation. All the interviews took place in an atmosphere of calm and co-operation. The conclusions which were then drawn up by the Office were acknowledged by the ILO Governing Body as useful and impartial.

In presenting these reports, the ILO does not limit itself to providing a mere description of the trade union and industrial relations situation, but makes a critical analysis which will clarify the current policies and practices in the countries concerned. The reports also propose solutions to existing problems and point to possible improvements related to the relevant ILO standards.

It is to my great satisfaction that the Governments, as well as the employers' and workers' organisations of the countries concerned, have recognised the usefulness of these studies in enabling them to acquire a better knowledge of the international labour Conventions and Recommendations, and in bringing up new ideas on the most effective ways of applying these instruments.

I should like to express my thanks for their valuable co-operation to the authorities of Spain and Yugoslavia, to the representatives of employers and workers and to all the persons who were good enough to receive members of the mission and to give freely of their time to participate in a true dialogue. Their appreciation of the value of the resulting studies is an invaluable source of encouragement to the ILO.

Francis BLANCHARD
Director-General
International Labour Office

FOREWORD

It is natural that freedom of association and, more generally, relations between heads of undertakings, organised labour and the public authorities should constitute a major theme in the thinking, analysis and debates of an organisation concerned exclusively with labour problems. The fact that the ILO is made up not only of government representatives but also of representatives of workers' and employers' organisations — in short its tripartite structure — can only strengthen its interest in these matters.

The principle itself of freedom of association is, of course, embodied in the constitutional texts of the ILO, which has also adopted very many international instruments on the subject. In particular, the Freedom of Association and Protection of the Right to Organise Convention, 1948 (No. 87), and the Right to Organise and Collective Bargaining Convention, 1949 (No. 98), establish basic standards in this field. A number of more recent instruments deal with specific aspects of the problem: the Workers' Representatives Organisations Convention, 1971 (No. 135) and Recommendation, 1971 (No. 143); the Rural Workers' Organisations Convention, 1975 (No. 141) and Recommendation, 1975 (No. 149); the Labour Relations (Public Service) Convention, 1978 (No. 151) and Recommendation, 1978 (No. 159); and the Collective Bargaining Convention, 1981 (No. 154) and Recommendation, 1981 (No. 163).

The Organisation has, in addition, set up machinery to supervise the application of international labour standards. Some of the procedures are general in scope: under the ILO Constitution, for instance, governments are required to submit reports regularly on the action taken to apply all Conventions ratified by them (article 22).[1] Technical review of the reports is entrusted to an independent body, the Committee of Experts on the Application of Conventions and Recommendations; later the reports are discussed at the tripartite level by a special committee set up each year by the International Labour Conference. The ILO has, moreover, established a special procedure for the protection of freedom of association, under an agreement with the United Nations Economic and Social Council; its application is entrusted to the Committee on Freedom of Association of the ILO Governing Body and, in exceptional cases, to a Fact-Finding and Conciliation Commission.[2]

In addition, the Second European Regional Conference (January 1974), in a unanimous resolution on freedom of association and industrial relations in Europe, called for studies "analysing in the most exhaustive manner possible the trade union situation and industrial relations existing within the framework of the various economic and social systems of the European countries in the light of the international standards adopted by the ILO in this field, as well as the experience acquired and data collected by the competent ILO bodies". The resolution recommended that "these studies should provide a basis, at a future session of the European Regional Conference or a meeeting specially convened for the purpose, for a wide exchange of views and experiences and for a frank and objective confrontation of ideas with a view to achieving better knowledge and understanding". The Third European Regional Conference (October 1979), in a resolution, also adopted unanimously, on freedom of association, trade union rights and industrial relations in Europe, invited the Governing Body to implement that recommendation.

The Programme and Budget for the biennium 1982-83 (Fifty-eighth Financial Period) accordingly provides for the undertaking of country studies of the trade union situation and industrial relations systems. These studies, it specifies, are to include an analysis of the legislation and factual situation of the countries concerned in the light of relevant ILO standards, as well as visits of ILO officials to those countries; they are then to be submitted for consideration and discussion to a tripartite working party appointed by the Governing Body. The studies and reports, together with the discussion on them, are then to be published. The International Labour Conference endorsed these proposals, along with the 1982-83 Programme and Budget as a whole, in a resolution adopted in June 1981, at its 67th Session.

The Spanish Government was among the first to invite the ILO to undertake a study of the trade union situation and industrial relations in the country. Other studies on the same subject were undertaken, one year prior to this one, in Hungary and Norway, and were submitted to the Governing Body at its 225th Session in February-March 1984. The study on Spain was conducted in parallel with another concerning Yugoslavia. It was carried out under the joint responsibility of Mr. Ian Lagergren, Chief of the International Labour Standards Department, since deceased, and Mr. Efrén Córdova, Chief of the Labour Law and Labour Relations Branch, since retired, with the collaboration, as in the case of the three other studies, of Mr. Jean-Michel Servais and, in this case, of Mr. Arturo Bronstein. The mission that visited the country from 27 November to 16 December 1983 consisted of Mr. Córdova, Mr. Servais and Mr. Bronstein, as well as Mr. Sanchez-Castaño who was responsible for administrative matters and documentation.

Notes

[1] They are also required to submit information on unratified instruments (article 19). The reports and information must be communicated to the representative national employers' and workers' organisations (article 23).

[2] See ILO: *ILO principles, standards and procedures concerning freedom of association* (Geneva, 2nd ed., 1978).

CONTENTS

Tables

ABBREVIATIONS

AISS	Social and Vocational Services Administration
CCOO	Trade Union Confederation of Workers' Committees
CEDA	Spanish Confederation of Autonomous Rights
CEOE	Spanish Confederation of Employers' Organisations
CEPYME	Spanish Confederation of Small and Medium-Sized Undertakings
CNT	National Confederation of Labour
CONFEMETAL	Organisation of employers in the metal trades
CSIF	Independent Trade Union Confederation of Public Servants
CSTC	Trade Union Confederation of Workers of Catalonia
ELA-STV	Solidarity Movement of Basque Workers
ETUC	European Trade Union Confederation
FETAP	Federation of Public Administration Workers
FTN	Confederation of Employers' Organisations of Catalonia (Fomento del Trabajo Nacional)
ICFTU	International Confederation of Free Trade Unions
INEM	National Employment Institute
INI	National Institute of Industries
INTG	National Trade Union Confederation of Galician Workers
IMAC	Mediation, Arbitration and Conciliation Institute
IOE	International Organisation of Employers
PSOE	Spanish Workers' Socialist Party
RENFE	National railways
SOC	Solidarity Movement of Catalan Workers
UGT	General Union of Workers
USO	Union of Workers' Trade Unions
WFTU	World Federation of Trade Unions
WCL	World Confederation of Labour

INTRODUCTION

1

In 1968, the ILO Governing Body instructed a study group to examine the labour and trade union situation in Spain. A mission visited the country and in the following year published its report.[1] Since that time, the country has experienced far-reaching political, social and economic changes. It was therefore particularly appropriate to review the industrial relations situation today and to analyse not so much the developments themselves but rather their outcome in Spain in the mid-eighties.

Of course, this does not mean that no reference has been made to the recent or more distant past: on the contrary, in many ways a brief reminder of past events has helped to throw light on the present. Moreover, relations between heads of undertakings, organised labour and the public authorities are part and parcel of a particular geographical, economic and cultural context, and it has been necessary to outline the salient features of that context; this has been done in Chapter 2. The study goes on to describe the employers' and workers' organisations, to trace their origins and to analyse their structure and methods of operation, their bargaining arrangements and disputes arising both out of industrial relations and relations of these organisations with the authorities, and other forms of worker participation in the undertaking.

In the process the study broaches topics which are today the subject of intense controversy in Spain. Not to do so has proved impossible, as these are vital issues, but every effort has been made throughout to maintain the utmost impartiality and objectivity. Great care has also been taken to look at the situation from an international standpoint and nothing in the following pages should be interpreted as laying down rights and wrongs or as siding with any particular party. In fact, the atmosphere during the meetings arranged by the mission was calm and the persons encountered generally took pains to explain their position on the most sensitive issues and to avoid entering into polemics.

As in the case of the previous studies, the members of the mission explained to the authorities before leaving Geneva how they wished to proceed. They particularly wanted to meet government representatives and leaders of employers' associations and trade unions, not only at the central level but also from various sectors of activity, as well as leading legal experts and academics. They also hoped to visit industrial and agricultural undertakings and establishments in the private and public sectors and to travel to various parts of the country. The provisional programme that the authorities then proposed faithfully reflected these concerns of the mission, which was able to make a number of additions, both in advance and on the spot.

The mission was received by the Minister of Labour and Social Security, Mr. Joaquín Almunia Amann, and by the Under-Secretary for Labour and Social Security, Mr. Segismundo Crespo Valera. It also met the Councillor for Labour of the Government Council *(Generalidad)* of Catalonia, Mr. Joan Rigoll Roig, the Vice-Councillor for Labour of the Basque Government, Mr. Humberto Cirarda Ortiz de Artiñano, and the Vice-Councillor for Labour, Industry and Social Security of Andalusia, Mr. José Antonio Guiñan.

The mission spoke with a large number of senior government officials, including the Technical Secretary-General of the Ministry of Labour and Social Security, Mr. Alvaro Espina, the Deputy Secretary-General for Labour, Mr. González de Lena, the Head of the Central Labour and Social Security Inspectorate, Mrs. María Luisa Senabre Llabata, the Director-General for Employment, Mr. Carlos Navarro, the Director of the National Employment Institute, Mr. Pedro Montero, the Director of the Spanish Institute of Emigration, Mrs. María Teresa Iza Echave, and the Provincial Directors for Labour and Social Security in Barcelona, Bilbao and Seville. It also talked to the Director of the Mediation, Arbitration and Conciliation Institute (IMAC), Mr. José Ignacio Moltó, the President of the Labour Relations Council of Andalusia, Mr. Rodriguez Piñero and the Secretary-General of the Labour Relations Council of the Basque country, Mr. Manuel Sendon Aranzamendi.

The mission visited the headquarters of the Spanish Confederation of Employers' Organisations (CEOE) where it held discussions with the then President of the Confederation, Mr. Carlos Ferrer Salat, and the former Secretary-General (and current President), Mr. José María Cuevas Salvador. It met the leaders of the Basque Confederation of Employers, the Centre of Basque Employers, the Confederation of Employers' Organisations of Catalonia *(Fomento del Trabajo Nacional — FTN)* and the Confederation of Andalusian Employers, as well as several officials of CONFEMETAL, the organisation of employers in the metal trades, and of the National Institute of Industries (INI).

The mission spoke to a large number of leaders of the General Union of Workers (UGT), both in Madrid and in Barcelona, Bilbao and Seville, and of the Metalworkers' Federation of the UGT. It met officials of the Trade Union Confederation of Workers' Committees (CCOO) in all four cities, and of its Metalworkers' Federation, and talked with the leaders of the Union of Workers' Trade Unions (USO), the Solidarity Movement of Basque Workers (ELA in Basque, STV in Spanish) and the National Trade Union Confederation of Galician Workers (INTG).

2

A meeting was arranged with the President and members of the Central Labour Tribunal, as well as two working meetings with a number of university professors, one in Madrid under the chairmanship of the Director of the Institute of Labour and Social Security Studies, Professor Jaime Montalvo Correa and the other in Seville under the chairmanship of Professor Miguel Rodríguez Piñero.

The mission visited several undertakings, both in Madrid and during its trip through the country: RENFE (railways), Biscaya steelworks, Rio Tinto explosives factory, SEAT (motor vehicles), posts and telecommunications, and a farm near Alcalá del Río, north of Seville. On each occasion, the group talked to members of the management as well as the works council and the trade unions that were represented.

At every stage of its visit, the mission encountered the same friendly atmosphere. Although the talks were sometimes protracted, the persons interviewed never showed any signs of impatience. They always replied clearly and courteously to the questions asked, even when they touched on highly sensitive issues. They also provided the documents, reports and statistics that were required. The members of the mission would here like to express their gratitude to all for the assistance given. They would like to extend special thanks to Mr. Carlos López Monis, Head of the Sub-Directorate General for International Social Affairs at the Ministry of Labour and Social Security, and to Mr. Mariano Gonzalez Herrera, Mr. Eustacio del Val and Mr. Alfredo Fernandez Barrio, Provincial Directors for Labour and Social Security in Bilbao, Barcelona and Seville respectively, who very kindly provided all the material assistance required for the organisation of the mission.

Note

[1] See ILO: *The labour and trade union situation in Spain* (Geneva, 1969); also published in *Official Bulletin* (Geneva, ILO), 1969, No. 4, Second Special Supplement.

SPAIN IN TRANSITION BETWEEN THE PAST AND THE FUTURE

2

HISTORICAL BACKGROUND

Spain's position at the south-western tip of Europe, set between the Atlantic and the Mediterranean and just over nine miles from Africa, has made it a crossroads of civilisations and the seat of one of the greatest empires the world has known.

The Phoenicians, Greeks and Carthaginians left their mark mainly on the Mediterranean shores of the peninsula. Rome then established centres of political and cultural influence, from which it was later to draw emperors and philosophers; the centuries of Roman colonisation brought Spain the Latin language, Roman law and the most advanced civilisation in Europe.

Early in the fifth century, the Suebi, the Alani, the Vandals and other barbarian peoples from the north occupied different parts of the peninsula. They were followed by another Germanic people, the Visigoths, who established their rule over the whole country, creating the first State on a national scale. Both the Latin and Visigothic influences seem to have been decisive factors in the shaping of the Spanish nation.

After 711, it was the turn of the Arabs who, during 700 years of rule, especially in Andalusia, profoundly influenced Spain's institutions, language and national character. However, the Arabs never exercised total control of Spain and for centuries the country remained divided up into many small Arab kingdoms and as many Christian principalities, whose fortunes varied with marriage alliances, dynastic successions and the hazards of war. For centuries, the Jewish Diaspora also found an asylum in Spain where it set up flourishing communities.

Throughout the Middle Ages, the Church, another vital component in the shaping of the national character, assumed an increasing role in the political and social life of Spain. Religious fervour, allied to the political will of a people who considered themselves heirs to the oldest indigenous traditions, the Roman and the Visigothic, gave impetus to a movement of reconquest and resettlement which ultimately spread to the confines of the Christian world. This movement

5

culminated in 1492 with the conquest of Granada, the last remaining Arab kingdom, and the expulsion of the Jews.

The end of the fifteenth century also saw the marriage of Isabella of Castille and Ferdinand of Aragon. The fusion of their two kingdoms brought about Spain's political unity and administrative centralisation, and combined Aragon's Mediterranean interests with Castille's new Atlantic ambitions.

This political unity did not, however, interfere with the local franchises *(fueros)*, under which the Crown acknowledged the right of some regions such as Aragon, Navarre, Catalonia and the Basque country to establish their own legal codes and tax systems. It also left intact the power of the Church, which reached its high point with the strengthening of the Inquisition, an ancient medieval institution which had already existed for a long time in other countries.

The fifteenth century marked an important stage in the country's linguistic development. Castilian, with its grammar now simplified and codified, was a medium in which literature could flourish. Such eminent novelists and playwrights as Cervantes, Lope de Vega and Calderón were later to write the masterpieces which make Castilian literature one of the most renowned in the Western world. However, other languages and dialects of the peninsula survived, especially in the north, where they still today reflect the Catalan, Basque and Galician identities.

During the next two centuries, under the sovereigns of the House of Austria, the Spanish monarchy achieved an unprecedented territorial expansion and took its place amongst the leading world Powers, especially under the reigns of Charles V and Philip II, when Spanish rule extended over the greater part of the Americas, Italy, the Netherlands, Franche-Comté, Roussillon and other European lands, and as far as the Philippines in the East. However, towards the end of this period, Spain gradually lost its European dependencies, while its military and colonial efforts overseas absorbed its human resources; its economy, entirely taken up with the mining of precious metals, turned away from industry, which delayed the advent of capitalism. It is therefore not surprising that, under the Bourbon dynasty which followed, some benevolent despots sought to renounce Spain's warlike adventures and to restore the economy. However, both dynasties were equally interested in the arts: in painting, the masterpieces of El Greco, Velazquez and Murillo, under the House of Austria, rivalled those of Goya under the Bourbons and, in architecture, the superb buildings of the Escorial and those of Burgos, Toledo and Seville date from these periods.

The fall of the Spanish empire in the Americas coincided in Spain with the Napoleonic invasion and the clash between two opposing concepts of national politics. The year 1812 saw, with the Cortes of Cadiz, the beginning of the confrontation between two ways of viewing Spanish society — one conservative, even absolutist, the other liberal and sometimes anti-clerical — which lasted until the end of the century. A dynastic crisis, caused by the abrogation of the Salic law in 1830, which had always prevented women from taking the throne, triggered the three bloody civil wars known as the Carlist Wars. Don Carlos, pretender to the throne against Queen Isabella II, found his strongest supporters in the rural areas of the Basque country, Navarre and Catalonia.

The first and most important stage in the Carlist Wars ended with the victory of the leader of the Isabellist forces and by the signing of the Convention of Vergara (1839). Thus began the long-standing influence of the military in Spanish politics. The Convention confirmed the franchises of the three regions mentioned above, but the honouring of this commitment fluctuated with the vagaries of Spanish politics.

The remainder of the nineteenth century saw a succession of military coups, plots and short-lived governments. This instability lasted until the accession to the throne of Alfonso XII and the Regency of his widow, Maria Christina of Habsburg. During this Regency, experienced politicians succeeded in establishing a stable constitutional system which lasted until the dictatorship of Primo de Rivero (1923); however, they were unable to suppress entirely the antagonisms between conservatives and liberals, Catholics and anti-clericals, moderates and radicals.

The industrialisation process, which started in Catalonia at the beginning of the nineteenth century, spread after 1850 to the rest of Spain, finding in Biscaya a second centre of development. An industrial proletariat soon arose, fired with a somewhat revolutionary ideology, whose struggles and organisations will be examined in the following chapter.

The Republic was proclaimed on two occasions, in 1873 and 1931. The first Republic was followed by the restoration of the Bourbons. The second Republic, characterised by grave social tensions and growing political polarisation, resulted in the Civil War of 1936-39. Spain still recalls with horror the loss of human lives and the passions unleashed during this period. Seen in an historical perspective and from the standpoint of the succession of constitutional and dictatorial regimes, sometimes civil, sometimes military, the Civil War is, in one sense, yet another manifestation, and a particularly tragic one, of the clash between the two deeply opposed concepts of Spanish society.

The Civil War ended with the victory of General Franco's armies. The provincial franchises were immediately abolished and the State confiscated the property of the two major trade union federations, the UGT (General Union of Workers) and the CNT (National Confederation of Labour). Franco set up an authoritarian and centralised regime which lasted until his death in 1975.

The last 15 years of Franco's regime saw large-scale industrial development, given impetus by foreign investment, currency brought in by mass tourism and cash sent home by Spanish migrant workers abroad. This industrialisation gave birth to a new working class and strengthened the middle classes; as a result, the general standard of living rose and the structure of Spanish society moved closer to that already achieved by countries industrialised at an earlier date.

After 39 years of dictatorship, a period of political and social upheaval might have been expected; however, the transition took place in an atmosphere of surprising calm and orderliness and, notwithstanding the restoration of freedoms, Spain did not experience the social disturbances which had been feared, and it avoided political pitfalls. In a 1978 referendum, the country approved a new and progressive Constitution; it welcomed social dialogue, held democratic elections at all levels and elected to Parliament in 1982 a socialist government with a large majority. However, at the end of 1983, it was faced with serious problems as a result of the world crisis, the radicalism of certain autonomous groups and terrorism in the Basque country.

GEOGRAPHY

The surface area of Spain is 504,750 square kilometres, making it the second largest country in Western Europe. Spanish territory covers five-sixths of the Iberian peninsula and two archipelagos, the Balearic Islands in the Mediterranean and the Canary Islands in the Atlantic. Continental Spain is bordered to the north by France (and the Principality of Andorra) and the Bay of Biscay, to the west and south-west by the Atlantic Ocean and Portugal and to the east and south-east by the Mediterranean Sea.

The geographical environment is said to have had an influence on the Spanish people and they, in their turn, have modified their surroundings. There is also reputedly a certain relationship between terrain and the national character. The habitat of Spain, with its wide open spaces and rugged mountains, its droughts and floods, its torrid heat and icy cold, its orchards and deserts, is unique amongst European countries. This is due not only to the difference between the continent and the islands, but also to the characteristics and contrasts which make up the topography of the peninsula: it has four shorelines — the Bay of Biscay, the Atlantic, the Gulf of Cadiz and the Mediterranean — each with different features, varying from the deep estuaries of the Atlantic to the sandy beaches of the Mediterranean; mountains cross the country from east to west in parallel ranges, from the Cantabrian mountains and the Pyrenees in the north to the Sierra Morena in the south; coastal ranges run parallel to the Mediterranean in Catalonia and in Andalusia, where the peaks of the Sierra Nevada are the highest in the peninsula; desolate plains and large basins form four catchment areas, the north and the west, where the main rivers flow into Portugal, and the south and the east, mainly consisting of the Basin of the Ebro, whose 12 tributaries water a considerable part of Spanish soil; finally, the dominant feature in Spanish topography, the great and overwhelmingly arid plateau of Castille, spreads over half the country.

This specific geographical setting, with its distinctive and contrasting aspects, helps us to understand the unity and diversity of Spain, which have been the two themes running through its history since earliest times.

THE SOCIO-ECONOMIC SITUATION

In 1983, the population of Spain was estimated to be 39 million. According to the National Institute of Emigration, there are a further 2,800,000 Spaniards living abroad, divided almost equally between Europe and America. It is estimated that during the past few years approximately 300,000 Spaniards have returned home. Also according to 1983 figures, more than 50 per cent of the population live in towns of more than 100,000 inhabitants.

At this date, there was an economically active population of 13,150,000 persons with a distribution by sector in line with the profile of a modern society: 17 per cent were employed in agriculture, 35 per cent in industry and 48 per cent in the services sector.

In December 1983, unemployment affected 17.8 per cent of the working population, i.e. a total of 2,335,000 persons.[1] According to information gathered by the National Employment Institute (INEM), about 600,000 of these unemployed workers were in search of their first job. In order to put the exact social situation into perspective, it should be added that households with several workers are very common in Spain.

Unemployment in Spain has been one of the highest in Europe and has continued to rise during the last few years, although its rate of increase slowed down by the end of 1983. Unemployment in 1983 rose in 40 out of 50 provinces; the highest unemployment rates in absolute figures were in Barcelona, Madrid, Seville and Valencia. As far as branches of activity are concerned, the building industry was the most affected by the rise in unemployment, both in relative and absolute terms, followed by engineering and the hotel industry.[2]

In spite of its high percentage, unemployment's social effects are partly compensated by a system of welfare and social security measures, which already existed or have been supplemented by the present Government; financial protection is generally provided on the basis of a dual scheme, contributory and non-contributory. Contributory compensation, proportional to the contributions paid during at least six months, may be as high as 80 per cent of the remuneration on which the worker has paid contributions during the preceding six months; this benefit is paid for a maximum period of 18 months. Although, in 1983, unemployment insurance covered only 30 per cent of those actually out of work, the Government envisaged taking steps to increase contributions and intimated that coverage would extend, in 1984, to 42 per cent of the unemployed.

At the time of the mission's visit to Spain, non-contributory compensation covered persons who found themselves once again unemployed and workers who had exhausted the possibilities of contributory protection. In some agricultural regions and especially in Andalusia and Extremadura, there was also protection against unemployment in the form of agricultural or community work, which some employers' and trade union circles qualified as socially unjustified and economically unviable. The Government was considering a rural employment programme aimed at replacing the community work system. This was to be implemented in 1984.

Other indirect measures seek to stimulate employment by making regulations on the subcontracting of manpower more flexible, by encouraging part-time work, by promoting early retirement — hence the setting up of the National Labour Protection Fund — and by altering the retirement age, which

9

has been reduced to 64 years in the mining industry; it is intended to generalise this retirement age in 1984. INEM was also seeking ways of reducing frictional unemployment by an improved distribution, throughout the country, of private and public employment possibilities. The Institute also operates 538 employment offices, situated in accordance with the number of persons seeking work; it has the monopoly in this field, because private employment agencies, including temporary work agencies, are forbidden in Spain.

After 1981, the seriousness of the unemployment situation (the rate was then 13.5 per cent) compelled the Government, the employers and the workers to take concerted action and conclude the National Employment Agreement, to which we shall refer in Chapter 5. Unfortunately, this concerted action did not produce the expected results and could not be repeated in the following years. Other concrete job-creating measures planned at the end of 1983, such as temporary contracts to launch new activities of indeterminate duration, have the backing of some but not all of the trade union organisations.

Outside the scope of these official measures and those taken by the social partners, Spain has seen a rapid expansion of underground work ("moonlighting") which, although it absorbs some of the unemployed, has serious economic and social drawbacks. Although it is impossible to give exact figures on the extent of this phenomenon, some estimate that it accounts for 6-8 per cent of the gross domestic product. It should also be added that this parallel economic activity goes hand in hand with tax evasion and infringement of labour legislation and is unfair competition to recognised enterprises, especially small- and medium-sized enterprises.

Alongside unemployment, there is the additional problem, just as serious, of inflation, which increased in 1983 by 12.2 per cent; although this percentage was lower than that of previous years, the inflation rate is still higher than in other European countries. The Government has therefore decided that in 1984, as a second priority after its fight against unemployment, it will bring inflation down to 8 per cent; to this end, it has fixed the maximum increase in wages in the public sector at 6.5 per cent, urged wage restraint in the private sector — without seeking to interfere in the free play of market forces — and planned other monetary and tax measures.

Inflation has deeply affected the pattern of industrial relations. As there is no real system of automatic wage indexing in Spain,[3] the unions have recourse to collective bargaining to try and defend workers' real wages against price increases. The aims of the basic agreements concluded at the national level in 1977 (the Moncloa Pact, signed by the political parties), in 1980 (Inter-Confederation Framework Agreement), in 1981 (National Employment Agreement) and in 1983 (Inter-Confederation Agreement) were, inter alia, to establish wage levels and wage increase limits designed to avoid spiralling inflation and protect the workers' purchasing power. Wages were also at the forefront of negotiations held at other levels, sometimes to the exclusion of any other issue. In preparation for the new round of negotiations to start in 1984, the major trade union federations and the employers' confederation had also drawn up strategies based on the levels of wage increases they were intending to claim or grant.

Faced with unemployment and inflation, the governments of the past few years have sometimes concentrated on anti-inflationary measures and at other times on employment programmes, without losing sight of the fact that the two policies influence each other; however, the Government has not restricted its action to measures relating to economic conditions or to corrective measures, but has aimed at tackling the heart of the problem. Aware of the basically structural nature of the problem and its relationship with the overall recession, the worsening of the national debt and the payments imbalance, the Government seems for some time to have been directing its strategy towards a general revival of the economy, more competitive export regulations and improved management of the public sector. Spain is also placing great hopes on its entry into the European Economic Community; negotiations have already been started on this subject and seem bound to continue for some time.[4]

At the beginning of the 1970s, Spain's average economic growth rate was 6 per cent. This rate abruptly slowed down in 1974 as a result of the energy crisis and then fell so low that from 1975 to 1982 the gross domestic product grew by only 1.6 per cent per year. According to the national employers' organisation, 276,000 undertakings, of which 50,800 employed wage earners, closed down between 1976 and 1982.[5] However, Spain could rely on its varied agriculture and a firmly established industrial base, which included the automobile industry, shipyards, the civil and military aircraft industry and the production of high technology railway equipment; it therefore possessed a potential for expansion and growth which the State, employers and workers sought to harness and modernise.

Modernisation took in particular the form of readaptation of industry, in other words, the reorganisation of certain key industries in which it was vital to make optimum use of means of production, to eliminate outmoded methods and systems and to introduce new technologies. In 1983, this conversion effort was aimed primarily at the iron and steel industry, shipbuilding and capital goods. As far as industrial relations were concerned, its immediate and most appreciable effect was to cut employment. Adjustments in the number of employees had almost been completed in many small- and medium-sized undertakings, but in some large undertakings in the public sector, and especially in the sectors mentioned above, negotiations were only beginning; although these measures should not affect more than some tens of thousands of workers in all, the fact that they are concentrated in several basic sectors of the economy has caused considerable tension. During the mission's visit to Spain, reconversion measures gave rise to strikes and demonstrations in the Ferrol shipyards and in the steelworks in Sagunto; in the latter town, there were violent clashes between the workers and police. The workers were afraid that the partial or total closure of the Mediterranean steelworks would result in massive dismissals which, they believed, might have been avoided by taking less radical measures. Discussions were also going on as to whether it was better to terminate or to suspend the contracts of affected workers while they were receiving benefits from the Employment Promotion Fund.

Elsewhere, reconversion was taking place normally. The mission visited another large iron and steel undertaking, the Biscaya Steelworks, and the SEAT car factory in Barcelona, where reconversion was taking place under conditions better accepted by those concerned. Other sectors had drawn up reconversion plans and set up application commissions to work out harmonious solutions which, endorsed by the 1983 Legislative Decree on industrial reconversion, made it possible, without imposing excessive hardship, to reduce staffing to a level corresponding to real production needs. Although there are still points of contention, the Government and the other social partners have done their utmost to resolve the problem by dialogue.

According to information obtained during the course of the mission, the serious economic difficulties which Spain is experiencing and the constant threat of a political crisis which could undermine the democratic system have had the unexpected effect of improving industrial relations in certain respects. Apart from several incidents on a limited scale, the negotiating partners, both workers and employers, and their rank and file showed an awareness of the country's critical situation and a readiness to combine their efforts to overcome it. On both sides, the leaders and the rank and file preferred negotiation to confrontation. The situation obviously serves as a catalyst to bring out a sense of social responsibility in the parties and to reduce signs of tension.

From a social viewpoint it should also be noted that 93 per cent of the population are literate and that the number of persons holding a university or secondary school diploma has increased considerably during the past ten years. Spain has many academic centres, including some employers' and trade union schools and institutes,[6] which offer a wide range of studies connected in various ways with labour issues. Evidence of this overall progress in education can be seen in the professional calibre and competence of employers' and trade union leaders and in the emergence of a new generation of practitioners who fulfil vital functions in industrial relations. The Spanish tradition of opening almost all key posts in the civil service to competition guarantees that the latter has a capable and qualified staff.

POLITICAL AND ADMINISTRATIVE ORGANISATION AND CONSTITUTIONAL PRINCIPLES

The first impression the mission had on examining the trade union and labour situation in Spain was that the country was enjoying civil freedoms and constitutional guarantees. This impression was formed by the media, especially by the press, but also as a result of the mission's daily contacts with occupational groups, the bargaining sessions it attended and its interviews with workers and employers. Added to this was the tangible feeling of pluralism which is very much alive in today's Spanish society. These two impressions, closely linked, reflect the reality of the basic values stressed in Article 1 of the Constitution, namely, liberty and pluralism. Other provisions of the preliminary part of the Constitution refer to political pluralism and the contribution made by workers' trade unions and employers' associations to the defence and promotion of their economic and social interests. The Constitution also recognises the rights of assembly, association and participation which, taken as a whole and applied in practice, contribute towards establishing a political and social framework in which freedom of association may be practised.

The Constitution of 1978 defines Spain as being a social and democratic State governed by the rule of law, with parliamentary monarchy as its political form. It is based on the indissoluble unity of the Spanish nation, "the common and indivisible country of all Spaniards", but recognises and guarantees the right to self-government of the nationalities and regions of which it is composed.

Although, historically, there were only three regional autonomous communities (Catalonia, Galicia and the Basque country), there are now 17, of which some, such as the Basque country, have their own Statute since 1979 which lays down the principles of their self-government. Apart from the regional autonomous communities, the territorial organisation of Spain is subdivided into provinces and municipalities, which also enjoy self-government for the management of their local affairs. There are at present 50 provinces and thousands of municipalities. As will be seen later in this report, provincial jurisdiction is a very important factor in collective bargaining.

Spain has therefore moved away from a strongly centralised form of government towards a pronounced decentralisation. This change has been accompanied by a gradual transfer of responsibilities, which has inevitably caused some administrative problems. Article 149 of the Constitution provides the State with exclusive jurisdiction over labour legislation, without prejudice to its execution by the agencies of the autonomous communities; article 150 stipulates, however, that the *Cortes Generales*, in matters of state jurisdiction, shall confer upon all or any of the autonomous communities the power to enact legislation for themselves within the framework of the principles, bases and guide-lines established by state law and that the State may transfer or delegate to the autonomous communities, through an organic law, powers belonging to it which by their very nature lend themselves to transfer or delegation.

The transfer of executive powers has taken place to a great extent in Andalusia, Galicia, Valencia and the Basque country. In the field of industrial relations, this transfer had already been carried out for various functions concerning trade union registration, co-operatives, collective bargaining, the settlement of disputes and the imposition of sanctions; this is also true for some aspects of individual labour relations (competence to make employment regulations was in the process of being transferred at the time the mission visited Spain).

In Galicia, for example, a Royal Decree of July 1982 provided that the Council of Galicia will perform certain functions in respect of collective agreements (when their territorial scope does not extend beyond the limits of Galicia), collective disputes, strikes, lock-outs, conciliation and arbitration and that some other functions, such as the keeping of employment statistics, will be jointly carried out by the State and the community. Earlier legislation had already transferred powers relating to administration and occupational safety and health. Other matters, such as migration, social security or higher inspection services, gave rise to too many problems or were considered non-transferable, in other words were deemed matters for the State's exclusive jurisdiction. During interviews with officials of the autonomous communities, the mission heard vastly differing opinions on the extent of transfers of power; some maintained that 95 per cent of functions in the field of employment, industrial relations and social security were transferable, whilst others were content with a much lower proportion. Different views were also held concerning the powers which some communities demand or that the central government grants, in the field of social legislation. This lack of agreement, if reflected in the definition of objectives and the application of principles, might cause discrepancies likely to complicate the future handling of industrial relations. Decentralisation will certainly enable communities to fill the gaps of State legislation and to make innovations and experiments, but it will also lead to jurisdictional disputes and delicate situations.[7]

It is curious that administrative decentralisation runs counter to a trend towards centralisation in collective bargaining and social dialogue which, for some years, have tended to be concentrated at the national level. These two trends are not necessarily incompatible, but the transfer of some of the State's powers of legislation might affect the viability or significance of central collective bargaining. Moreover, while the central Government is in favour of the autonomy of the social partners, some autonomous communities seem more disposed towards state intervention. Some officials and employers' leaders expressed the fear that too much autonomy might finally undermine the unity and mobility of the employment market.

The Ministry of Labour nevertheless retains the key position in the complex executive system currently being developed. These central services include the Under-Secretariat, the General Technical Secretariat and several regional directorates, including those of labour and of general inspection services, both of which fulfil particularly vital functions in the field of industrial relations. The labour administration also comprises provincial offices and some autonomous institutes; however, the provincial offices will have to cede their power to the government councils and other bodies being set up at present in the communities. Some of the government councils already set up, such as the *Generalidad* of Catalonia, take initiatives and carry out studies which would formerly have been functions of the central administration; some industrial relations boards, such as that in Andalusia, seem prepared to assume their new powers, whereas others are still in the process of examining the various opportunities which autonomy affords them.

The three most important autonomous institutes are the National Employment Institute (INEM), the Spanish Institute of Emigration and the National Institute of Industries (INI), whose functions are quite closely connected with industrial relations. The National Mediation, Arbitration and Conciliation Institute (IMAC), set up in 1979, might play a vital role in industrial relations, but was not yet in a position to carry out all its functions at the time of the mission's visit to Spain. The considerable amount of research and information work carried out by the Institute of Labour and Social Security Studies, attached to the Ministry of Labour, should also be mentioned.

CHARACTERISTICS OF THE SYSTEM

The new constitutional system also brought about another basic change which could already be detected in 1976, namely the shift from state decision to more autonomous decision-making in industrial relations. Spain has thus moved away from a strict interventionism, under which its industrial relations had been regulated by decree, regulations and arbitration without appeal, to a voluntary system. Indeed, the Constitution grants the social partners the power to act, negotiate and decide on any matters concerning their economic and social interests and concerning relations established in this respect; it makes freedom of association a basic right and acknowledges the right of collective bargaining, as well as the binding character of agreements; workers enjoy the constitutional right to strike in defence of their interests.

The voluntarist tendencies of the Constitution were further extended by the Workers' Charter, approved in 1980, which has its origins in the Constitution itself. Some traces of interventionism which remained in the Charter were later removed by the Constitutional Court, which will be further discussed later in this report. Although it has not relinquished its role of regulator and prime mover in the field of social policy, the State nevertheless leaves it to the social partners to settle their own affairs.

The Workers' Charter was followed in 1980 by the revision of the Act on Labour Procedures and by the Basic Act respecting employment (1980), and by further provisions designed primarily to promote employment and to protect unemployed workers. However, it was only in 1984, with the adoption by Parliament of the Organic Act on Freedom of Association, that the legislature gave attention to the overall and specific regulation of collective labour relations. Meanwhile, the Miners' Charter and other texts regulating individual and collective labour relations for specific categories of workers had been adopted. It was also planned to introduce charters for public servants and other groups of workers. The Workers' Charter specified five employment relationships of a special nature which should be regulated by appropriate decrees: work in the service of a family, the work of convicts in penitentiaries, the work of professional sportsmen, the work of public entertainers and the work of persons involved in commercial operations for the account of one or more employers. It was therefore not possible to judge at that stage whether labour legislation was tending towards a uniform system or towards a system of sector-based industrial relations.

Apart from the Constitutional Court, the Labour Court, highly respected in the country, holds an important position in the system of industrial relations. Its functions are limited in principle to the settlement of legal disputes — individual or collective — and it deals only rarely with conflicts of interests. Nevertheless, both the Constitutional Court and the Labour Court assume functions of interpreting the law and providing practical guidance which go far beyond the letter of their mandate. Some of the Spanish lawyers whom the mission met stressed the significance of certain recent judgements and mentioned that there was a tendency to leave to the judges the regulation of industrial relations.

In addition to changing direction, labour legislation is apparently tending to extend its field of application. Sectors previously excluded are now contained in this field of application and contribute to further developing collective labour relations.[8] Although the trade unions and employers' associations remain the major protagonists, recent years have seen the emergence of other groups which are also claiming their rights in this field; the most active are probably public servants, technicians and middle management, who either join the general trade union movement or set up their own organisations. The question of public servants will be dealt with in Chapter 8. As regards professionals, middle management and technicians, there has recently been a change in their general attitude: whereas previously they felt closer to the employers, many are now siding with the workers.

Spain is also noteworthy for having evolved new types of professionals, such as social studies graduates who are involved in consultancy and industrial relations management, in staff management and in social security.[9] During the past few years, the professions of labour lawyer and personnel manager have developed particularly.

Another new trend is apparent in industrial relations: a determination to promote social dialogue and consultation which, though adumbrated in the Constitution, has developed outside the established structures. The Constitution provided that an act should set up a council composed of representatives of the trade unions and other industrial organisations to advise the Government on the drawing up of programmes. This council has not yet been established and consultation has developed spontaneously by means of agreements discussed and concluded by the trade unions and industrial associations, with or without government representation.

At the enterprise level, the Constitution provides that the public authorities shall promote effectively the various forms of participation and take measures to facilitate the access of workers to ownership of the means of production. However, there is as yet no act to implement these principles, nor are there federal agreements to define the specific forms of participation. As will be seen later, collective bargaining is the vehicle for workers' participation in the decisions of enterprises. The PSOE (Spanish Workers' Socialist Party), at present in power, advocates in its electoral programme "increasing the workers' right of collective bargaining and their institutional representation and participation in management, so that they may participate in decision-making on matters of general economic policy".[10]

Finally, industrial relations are characterised in Spain by the influence of non-occupational factors. In spite of the conciliatory spirit which has so far always prevailed in difficult moments, there is quite a strong politicisation in the relationships between workers and employers, which is also reflected in the frequency of disputes.

As a result, the system of industrial relations has been evolving on the basis of the 1978 Constitution or the texts drawn up by the legislators in 1980; it has also been shaped by jurisprudence and to an even greater extent by the normal development of a system in which the two partners have regained their freedom of action. At the time of the mission's visit to Spain, the system was in transition; several organic or ordinary acts [11] were at the preparatory stage or being planned. From the institutional standpoint, several structural elements were still lacking and the final outlines of the system had still not yet been drawn. Although the present report takes into account the main changes which have since occurred, it nevertheless describes a particular stage in, rather than a final picture of, the Spanish system of industrial relations.

SPAIN AND THE INTERNATIONAL LABOUR STANDARDS ON FREEDOM OF ASSOCIATION AND INDUSTRIAL RELATIONS

As a very experienced Spanish observer recently wrote:

It would be hard to find a country in which the ILO is as well known or as highly thought of as it is in Spain. Any important event in the labour field invariably elicits mention of the ILO. Sometimes Spanish commentators are concerned only to cite relevant international labour standards; more often they invoke the ILO's moral authority by expounding what they believe to be its policy on a particular point.[12]

Spain is, in fact, the country which has ratified the most international labour Conventions (107 on 31 January 1984). Amongst these must be cited, because they concern freedom of association and industrial relations: the Right of Association (Agriculture) Convention, 1921 (No. 11), the Freedom of Association and Protection of the Right to Organise Convention, 1948 (No. 87), the Right to Organise and Collective Bargaining Convention, 1949 (No. 98), the Workers' Representatives Convention, 1971 (No. 135), the Rural Workers' Organisations Convention, 1975 (No. 141), and the Labour Relations (Public Service) Convention, 1978 (No. 151).

Spain has also ratified the International Covenant on Economic, Social and Cultural Rights and the International Covenant on Civil and Political Rights adopted by the United Nations, as well as the European Social Charter.[13]

During its 1983 Session, the ILO Committee of Experts on the Application of Conventions and Recommendations made observations concerning the application by Spain of Convention No. 87 (ways in which the right to strike are granted) and of Convention No. 98 (extension of collective agreements); these matters will be discussed later in the report. Furthermore, many allegations have been submitted to the Committee on Freedom of Association of the Governing Body of the ILO — mainly since 1956, in which year Spain rejoined the ILO (of which it is a founding member); these too will be referred to later in the report. Finally, the Governing Body of the ILO instructed a Study Group in 1968 to examine the labour and trade union situation in Spain; after having visited the country, the mission published an extensive report.[14]

Ratified international treaties, once they have been officially published in Spain, form part of the internal legal order; their provisions may be repealed, amended or suspended only in the manner provided for in the treaties themselves or in accordance with the general rules of international law.[15] Furthermore, the articles of the Spanish Constitution concerning fundamental rights and liberties must be interpreted in conformity with the Universal Declaration of Human Rights and the international treaties and agreements ratified by Spain.[16] Eminent jurists informed the mission that the Constitutional Court, as well as the other courts, are influenced to a considerable extent in their deliberations by international labour Conventions and comments put forward on this basis by the competent bodies of the ILO; this also holds true for theoretical writing on labour matters; furthermore, these instruments serve as terms of reference in the conclusion of collective agreements.

Notes

[1] *Boletín de Estadísticas Laborales* (Madrid, Ministry of Labour and Social Security), No. 1, Dec. 1983, p. 1.

[2] ibid., pp. 11-14.

[3] ILO et al.: *La indiciación de los salarios* (Madrid, H. Blume Ediciones, 1981), p. 204.

[4] In 1985, the date of Spain's entry into the European Economic Community was fixed at 1 January 1986.

[5] *Boletín de la Confederación Española de Organizaciones Empresariales*, No. 53, Sep. 1983, p. 12.

[6] The role of the workers' universities mentioned in paragraphs 702-704 of the report of the Study Group which visited Spain in 1969 has been reduced and they are now mainly concerned with vocational training.

[7] Luis Enrique de la Villa: *Panorama de las relaciones laborales en España* (Madrid, Editorial Tecnos, 1983), p. 15.

[8] L. M. Almansa Pastor: "Los sujetos del derecho del trabajo y la seguridad social", in *Revista de Trabajo* (Madrid), Nos. 63 and 64, 3rd and 4th quarters, 1981, p. 23.

[9] At present there are 30,000 social science graduates; 10,000 of these are members of professional associations.

[10] See paragraph 5 of the chapter on "The economic crisis and employment".

[11] According to the Constitution, the regulations pertaining to basic rights such as freedom of association and the right to strike must be the subject of organic laws, which must be adopted by an absolute majority of the members of the Congress (Chamber of Deputies).

[12] J. Albalate Lafita: "The influence of international labour Conventions on labour law and social change in Spain", in *International Labour Review* (Geneva, ILO), July-Aug. 1979, pp. 443-457.

[13] When ratifying the Charter, the Spanish Government declared that Spain would interpret and apply Articles 5 and 6 of the Charter in relation with Article 31 and the Appendix,

so that their provisions might be compatible with those contained in Articles 28 (the right to join a trade union and the right to strike), 37 (the right to collective bargaining and collective labour dispute measures), 103, section 3 (status of public officials) and 127 (magistrates), of the Spanish Constitution.

[14] See ILO: *The labour and trade union situation in Spain* (Geneva, 1969).

[15] See article 96 of the Constitution.

[16] Article 10 of the Constitution.

EMPLOYERS AND TRADE UNIONS

3

AN EVENTFUL SOCIAL HISTORY

Brotherhoods and guilds were for centuries, in Spain as in many other European countries, the only type of occupational organisation. The first workers' associations, in the modern sense, appeared in 1840. They most often took the form of mutual aid societies or co-operatives, the only associations whose establishment was authorised. Nevertheless, trade unions were also formed, in particular in Catalonia, where there was already a high concentration of industry.

The year 1855 was one of serious social tension in Barcelona. Several strikes and lock-outs had already occurred when, on 2 July, the first general strike in Spanish history was called. The conflict paralysed the life of the city and troops occupied the factories. The strikers demanded the free exercise of the right to organise, with a slogan that has remained famous: "association or death". During this period other regions also witnessed social struggles which sometimes took a serious, even violent, turn. It was only in 1868, however, at the end of the Civil War that led to the dethronement of Isabella II, that freedom of association was recognised.

The Spanish workers' movement developed in a notable manner. Followers of Bakunin were the instigators of a libertarian current which was to leave a lasting mark on the social history of the country, while Paul Lafargue, the son-in-law of Marx, organised a movement along socialist lines. By 1872, the break between the anarchists on the one hand and the socialists on the other was complete, a split which certainly delayed the development of Spain's nascent trade union movement.

Faithful to their doctrine, and probably also to circumvent the bans imposed by the Government, the anarchist leaders for a long time refused to create a centralised structure: partial or general strikes that relied on the solidarity of the working masses appeared to them to be the best way to obtain their revolutionary objectives. They did not found the National Confederation of Labour (CNT) until 1910. By contrast, the General Union of Workers (UGT), a centralised and socialist-inspired organisation, came into being in 1888, shortly after the adoption in 1887 of the Associations Act. The PSOE, with which it always had close links, had been founded under a slightly different name a few years previously (1879). Among the founders of both organisations was the leading figure of Pablo Iglesias (1850-1925). The purpose of the UGT, according to its rules, was to improve the situation of its members by means of strikes, but also by intervening in public life side by side with the socialist party in favour of the adoption of labour legislation.

Furthermore, the papal encyclical *Rerum novarum* (1891) gave rise to the first Catholic-inspired groups which were particularly successful in rural areas; the encyclical was also at the origin of the creation in 1911 of the Solidarity Movement of Basque Workers *(Solidaridad de Trabajadores Vascos)*, an organisation that became firmly established in the workers' community which it sought to defend.

A number of independent trade unions were also created from 1918 onwards, but these were held in low regard by the other trade union organisations because of the support they received from employers and the public authorities.

However, the CNT and the UGT proved to be the most powerful trade union confederations. The anarchist confederation was particularly well established in Catalonia and Andalusia, and played a decisive part in the strikes and revolts which shook Spain from 1910 onwards. The Government became concerned and used the various means of repression provided by the law: suspension of constitutional guarantees, trial under the provisions of the Penal Code relating to illegal associations, proclamation of a state of emergency. The CNT was practically outlawed as a national organisation.

The UGT, together with the majority of trade union organisations, was dissolved by the Government during the general strike of 1911. The measure failed, however, to have any lasting effect. The socialist confederation developed particularly in the northern and central areas of the country. At its 1918-19 congress, it considerably amended its objectives and means of action, proclaiming the class struggle as its fundamental doctrine, establishing its political and religious neutrality and demanding control of production and management of undertakings with a view to their socialisation or nationalisation.

The development and growing influence of the trade unions incited employers' circles to organise too. Abandoning their initial groups that were religious in nature, they formed the Spanish Employers' Confederation which, from 1911 onwards, co-ordinated the action of all the employers' associations. These associations adopted the same tactics as their trade union adversaries: they ordered more and more partial or general lock-outs, intervened increasingly in trade union struggles in order to maintain divisions and provoke rifts, launched attacks against certain governments accused of encouraging the workers' movement and even appealed to the police and military authorities to take action. The tough attitude which they adopted in the social struggles was certainly not unrelated to the very widespread sentiment in employer circles during the troubled period from 1917 to 1922 that it was necessary to ward off what they saw as the imminent threat of revolution.[1]

As of 1923 the social situation reflected the disruptions and uncertainties of the political life of the country. The Directory formed by General Miguel Primo de Rivera in 1926 established an occupational organisation of a national corporative character that brought about extensive state intervention in all collective labour relations; it did not, however, alter the previous status of the trade unions. The proclamation of the Republic in 1931 gave fresh impetus to the UGT, whose membership was now over a million workers, and to the CNT, with 1,200,000 members.[2] The UGT was closely associated with government action during the early years of the new regime through various socialist ministers. The CNT, meanwhile, one branch of which — eventually to become the dominant force — was all in favour of immediate revolutionary action, seized every opportunity to call a general strike. The early years of the Republic also witnessed the establishment of the unions of the National Syndicalist Action Groups.

The insurrection faced by the coalition government formed by the radicals, the Spanish Confederation of Autonomous Rights (CEDA) and the agrarian movement in 1934 began with a call for a general strike. Asturias was the centre of resistance by workers (UGT and CNT) against the armed forces; there were approximately 2,000 deaths and more than 40,000 arrests; some union leaders went underground for a certain time. The UGT, but not the CNT which remained faithful to its anarchist strategy of refusing all forms of collaboration with the State, took part in 1936 in the formation of a Popular Front with a large number of left-wing parties, which won the elections of 16 February 1936. On 18 July, civil war broke out.

In the areas occupied by the nationalists, the first measures were soon taken that were to lead to the repeal of the trade union legislation in force, the dissolution of the existing workers' organisations and the confiscation of their assets, which were turned over to the Falange Party and the National Syndicalist Action Groups.

The Government of General Franco introduced a system of occupational organisations whose essential principles were laid down in a Labour Charter adopted in March 1938. The system was based on a "national syndicalist community". All citizens participating in production as workers or employers became members, according to branch of activity or service, of "vertical trade unions", i.e. single corporative organisations of employers and workers, with a graduated structure under the direction of the State: affiliation and payment of contributions were compulsory. Any attempt to establish occupational associations outside this organisation constituted an offence under the Penal Code. The administrative authority was entrusted with the regulation of collective labour relations: the Ministry of Labour enacted regulations, by sector of activity (or even for a single undertaking of particular importance), which laid down minimum labour standards. Collective agreements were banned, at least until 1958, when the legislation was amended on this point.

The Committee on Freedom of Association of the ILO's Governing Body stressed on several occasions the fundamental contradiction between the legislation then enforced and the principles of freedom of association.[3] It also pointed out that the legislation on strikes could be interpreted as providing for their absolute prohibition, in the case of all workers and not only in the case of workers engaged in essential services.[4] The ILO Committee of Experts on the Application of Conventions and Recommendations adopted similar conclusions, in particular on the occasion of a general survey of freedom of association and collective bargaining.[5]

Alongside the official "syndicalist" organisation, membership of which was in principle compulsory for all workers, the various currents within the historical trade union movement sought to maintain their presence in the country, in particular in the highly industrialised regions. These were difficult times as their activities were at the time against the law and had to be conducted underground.

The UGT was able to reorganise abroad where it benefited from international trade union solidarity, principally from the member organisations of the International Confederation of Free Trade Unions (ICFTU). Despite the repression endured by union activists, the UGT managed to retain a significant amount of influence, particularly in the Basque country and the Asturias, which had previously been its strongholds.

The leaders of the CNT were also the target of repressive measures by the Government, and their efforts to re-establish the Confederation met with failure on a number of occasions.

In the Basque country, meanwhile, the ELA-STV succeeded in maintaining contact with its rank-and-file members: it was able, for example, to have some of its members elected as official trade union delegates. It also received the active support — moral and financial — of the international trade union movement.

Several other workers' organisations were established during this period. Particular mention should be made of the Union of Workers' Trade Unions (USO) created at the beginning of the 1960s by members of Catholic movements.

In addition, 1956 saw the beginnings of a new phenomenon, temporary at first and then on a more permanent basis as from 1964, in the Asturias, Viscaya, Madrid and subsequently elsewhere: groups of workers in certain undertakings began to appoint delegates responsible for presenting grievances or claims to the management. Eventually, these contacts developed into actual negotiations. These "Workers' Committees" opted to act within the law and, for instance, put forward candidates at official trade union elections, some of whom were elected and even occupied responsible posts. This was the policy of what was termed "*entrismo*" (penetration) in Spain, as opposed to, for example, that of the UGT, which refused any form of participation in the official trade union movement. The Workers' Committees held assemblies and set up co-ordinating committees at higher levels. They claimed to have no political, trade union or religious ties whatsoever, but it seems clear that from the beginning they were composed above all of communist militants (the majority) and workers from Catholic backgrounds.

Even though the representatives of the Workers' Committees were at times tolerated to some extent by the authorities, the leaders and members of all the above-mentioned trade union movements were frequently prosecuted for offences such as illegal association, illegal propaganda, publication of clandestine printed matter, holding of illegal meetings or demonstrations or other acts regarded as law-and-order offences. A substantial number of union leaders at the time were tried summarily by ordinary courts or by special courts such as the Law and Order Court. Many people claimed, moreover, that the detainees were subjected to ill-treatment.

The investiture of King Juan Carlos I in the autumn of 1975 marked the beginning of a progressive but rapid liberalisation of the regime. The trade unions quickly emerged from the underground. An Act recognising freedom of association was adopted on 1 April 1977; a few days later, Spain ratified ILO Conventions Nos. 87 and 98, the basic international instruments on the subject. As stated in the preceding chapter, the new Constitution, which came into force in the last days of 1978, embodies the essential principles of an entirely different system of industrial relations.

EMPLOYERS' ASSOCIATIONS

With the reappearance of trade union confederations, employers began to feel the need to form associations outside the corporative organisation, which was destined to disappear. The conclusion in October 1977, at the Moncloa Palace, of an agreement between the Government and the main parties represented in Parliament, which defined the basic principles of a financial, economic and social policy but from which the employers (as well as the trade unions) were excluded, merely encouraged the movement, the mission was told.

Although there are exceptions, especially in Catalonia, the employers' associations established at that time have in principle no connection with those existing before the Civil War. On the other hand, the mission was informed that the new federations and confederations had frequently evolved out of the "employers' unions" which had operated during the Franco era within the corporative organisation and membership of which had been compulsory. Managers of undertakings were thus able to retain, in a different form, the organisational set-up established by the previous regime — a fact which, according to some people, would seem at least partly to explain the exceptionally large membership of employers' associations. In fact, the majority of undertakings are members of such associations: at the time of the mission, the CEOE claimed to represent over 1,300,000 undertakings employing approximately three-quarters of the wage-earning population. According to a survey carried out in 1982 of 262 undertakings employing more than 500 workers (a total of 730,000 to 740,000 workers), about 70 per cent were members of the CEOE.[6]

It was in June 1977 that the employers' associations joined together to form the CEOE, which is composed both of federations by branch of activity (the majority) and of territorial organisations, individual undertakings often being members of both. Statistically speaking, of 143 confederations affiliated to the CEOE in 1982 101 were sectoral and 42 territorial organisations. The CEOE also had three associated organisations, including the Spanish Confederation of Women Managers. The branch federations may in turn be made up of regional and sectoral unions (i.e. representing a particular sector within the branch, such as jewellery in the metal trades). This is true, in the case of the iron and steel industry, of CONFEMETAL, the largest member federation of the CEOE, created in 1978 by a merger between two organisations.

The CEOE embraces industry, commerce and agriculture. Its affiliates include the Spanish Confederation of Small and Medium-Sized Undertakings (CEPYME), which operates at the regional and national levels and is in a separate category within the employers' organisation.

Many regional employers' organisations have also joined the CEOE. Particular mention should be made of the powerful FTN in Catalonia, which dates back to 1771 and whose sense of tradition is reflected in the venerable premises where its leaders hold their meetings. In the Basque country, the mission met the leaders of two employers' organisations which are rivals, at least as far as Viscaya is concerned: the General Confederation of Employers of Viscaya and the Centre of Basque Employers. Both are, however, affiliated to the CEOE, the first directly, the second through its members. It also met the leaders of the Confederation of Employers of Andalusia, which was created in 1979 and also has close relations with the CEOE. They explained that CEPYME is an integral part of the Confederation, just as it is of the CEOE at the national level. They also emphasised the specific problems of employers in the agricultural sector.

The CEOE is itself affiliated to the International Organisation of Employers (IOE). It has opened a permanent liaison office with the European Communities in Brussels, where it is extremely active. It has generally strengthened its presence at the international level and undertaken numerous missions in Europe and elsewhere (particularly in Latin America).

The CEOE's objective is to promote private initiative and the market economy. It should in fact be noted that the Spanish Constitution recognises free enterprise within the framework of the market economy; it adds that the public authorities guarantee and protect its exercise and the safeguarding of productivity in accordance with the demands of the economy and, as the case may be, of its planning.[7] A further purpose of the CEOE is to represent the general and common interests of employers vis-à-vis society, the administration and workers' organisations. Its functions therefore fall within both the social and the economic fields.

The structure of the employers' confederation is defined in its by-laws. The supreme body is the General Assembly, which brings together the representatives of all its members. It meets in plenary session but also has a standing committee, which is composed of slightly under half of the Assembly's members (together with the members of the executive committee) and is called upon to deal with certain questions specified in the rules. The executive committee is a collegiate body composed of some 60 members which elects an executive board (of 18 persons) operating on a permanent basis.

The CEOE also has committees, established either on a temporary or on a more permanent basis, which examine problems in a particular sector (commerce, tourism, transport) or a specific field (economics, labour relations), in some cases through subcommittees entrusted with a particular issue (energy, technology, taxation, collective bargaining, disputes and arbitration, vocational training, etc.); the committees formulate proposals for action and submit them to the competent bodies of the Confederation.

Lastly, the Confederation has a secretariat whose competence is recognised by all, whether in regard to substantive problems (economic and fiscal matters, industrial relations, etc.) or problems of management, public relations and communications (its press service is highly reputed). The Confederation regularly publishes books and reports on economic and social affairs.

The leaders of the CEOE explained that the organisation has pursued a policy of dialogue with the other social forces. As will be seen later, the CEOE has in the last few years participated in the conclusion of inter-occupational collective agreements applying to the whole country. This practice, together with the development of consultation with the Government on social issues, has certainly consolidated the role of the Confederation's central bodies. Even when discussions are not held at the higher level, the task of the central bodies is not inconsiderable: they take part in strategy planning through meetings with employers' representatives engaged in negotiations, offer advice and provide support. If a member association wishes to exceed the standards contained in collective agreements of broader scope, it takes the necessary steps (in conjunction with the national trade union organisation) to ensure compliance with the agreement reached. The mission was told that this kind of pressure on members was proving to be increasingly effective. Nevertheless, affiliates are not always sufficiently informed about the agreements in force, though a considerable effort is now being made to provide them with all the necessary documentation.

Without going into the details of the specific characteristics of the Spanish undertaking, which would go far beyond the scope of this study, mention should be made of two features which appear to have a direct bearing on industrial relations. Firstly, as the CEOE leaders pointed out, 92 per cent of undertakings employed fewer than 500 workers; the possible repercussions of this on the extent of trade union membership will be discussed elsewhere.

Secondly, a substantial number of undertakings are owned or controlled by the State. Many are members of a holding company, the INI; the CEOE is in fact in favour of their affiliation and many have become members of employers' federations in particular branches of activity and, through them, of the CEOE; these undertakings do not, however, sit on the Confederation's executive bodies. Although their rate of membership of the CEOE is high — about 50 per cent — it remains well below that of private undertakings.

TRADE UNIONS

A multiple trade union system

Several rival trade unions coexist in Spain. The historical reasons for this situation have been mentioned; there are also reasons arising out of different conceptions of trade unionism, different choices of society and, lastly, different political affinities — though all confederations deny having any structural links with political parties. This is the case, in particular, of the two main trends within the Spanish trade union movement.

The UGT has always appeared to be a sister organisation of the PSOE: reference has already been made to their long common history. Its principal leaders are apparently members of the Party; some are on the PSOE's executive body and some are socialist deputies in the Cortes. In addition, the mission was informed, worker members of the Party are expected to join the UGT. Even though relations between them may not be institutionalised, informal meetings are frequent. It is true, none the less, that the UGT has on more than one occasion adopted a critical attitude towards the policy of the socialist Government. This occurred during the mission's visit in connection with the controversial issue of industrial redeployment.

Similarly, though the Workers' Committees, which have formed their own confederation (the CCOO), are by statute independent of all political parties and though various tendencies are in fact apparent among them, it is generally recognised that the majority of their leaders and their most active militants are very close to the Spanish Communist Party. Almost all the members of the Confederation's executive committee seem to be Party members and the Secretary-General of the CCOO has been a member of the Party's political bureau; a number of the Confederation's leaders have also been elected to Parliament on the Party's lists.

The USO claims to defend the objectives of a politically independent form of trade unionism whose origins are to be found in the principles of Christian social doctrine and which at one time was in favour of self-management.

Lastly, the anarchist trade union movement, which is in fact divided into several tendencies, has failed, as will be seen later, to recapture the kind of appeal that it once had.

The reason for the existence of so many trade union movements is also to be found in the nationalist sentiment of certain regions. Among the unions established on nationalist lines is the ELA-STV, already referred to, which is considered to be very close to the Basque Nationalist Party. There is also the National Trade Union Confederation of Galician Workers (INTG), which was founded recently (1977). In addition, even if it appears to be appreciably less important, a Trade Union Confederation of Workers of Catalonia (CSTC) was recently established by several union organisations in the region, including the Solidarity Movement of Catalan Workers (SOC).[8]

Trade union membership

A further characteristic of Spanish trade unionism appears to be the low rates of affiliation; while it is always a delicate task to make estimates and while the figures vary according to the sources used — about 25 per cent at the time of writing according to some, 15-17 per cent according to others — it is generally recognised that rates of membership have fallen considerably in the last few years. Membership is in any case well below that of the 1930s, and is among the lowest in Europe. Women's participation in the trade union movement also appears to be low. All agree, however, that the level of trade union membership is appreciably higher in the Basque country; in Bilbao, some explain this by the Basques' readiness to form associations (the co-operative movement is also stronger in that region). By contrast, the mission was informed that the rate of membership was particularly low in Navarre.

The mission asked union leaders, among other things, why the rate of affiliation was so low. Many mentioned the existence in undertakings of forms of workers' representation outside the trade union movement: staff meetings, staff delegates and works committees, which will be discussed later on. In their view (though their criticism was not shared by all currents of trade union opinion), staff delegates and works committees performed a number of functions, such as the negotiation of collective agreements, which should rightfully be carried out by the trade unions and thus consolidate the trade unions' role in regard to the workers. Moreover, several union officials referred to the disinclination of many employers to allow union activities, outside the so-called autonomous representation, within the undertaking.[9] The UGT leaders added that the purpose of the new provisions of the trade union Act then being drafted was precisely to correct this situation and to enhance the role of union sections and representatives.

The mission was also told that few workers join trade unions because they have no immediate interest in doing so, as collective agreements apply even to those who do not pay union dues; hence, the controversial issue has arisen of whether non-union workers should pay a "solidarity contribution". As will be seen, the reply to this question varies from union to union.

Furthermore, some considered that the structure of the Spanish economy, with its predominance of small and medium-sized undertakings, was itself not conducive to unionisation, if only because the work centres are so widely scattered.

There was also the feeling that the workers expected far too much from the advent of a free trade union system and that they were rather too ready to believe that the free trade unions would solve all their problems. Their disillusionment was bound to be accentuated by the economic crisis and the employment situation, whose effect on the rate of membership was emphasised.

There was also a definite link, the mission was told, between the low membership rate and the precarious financial situation of most Spanish trade union organisations. As will be seen, the unions are too poor to pay for a large number of permanent officials or launch major publicity campaigns; at the same time, low membership means a low level of contributions, the main source of income for a union. In addition, the check-off system, which is a more reliable source of revenue than voluntary contributions or union stamps, is not very widespread. This precarious situation has further aggravated the problem of how to distribute the assets of the previous regime's corporative trade union organisation, a question which is dealt with in the next chapter. For lack of funds the unions also find it difficult to offer the legal, social and other services which the corporative organisation used to provide, another factor that may discourage people from joining a union.

Lastly, several of the persons spoken to, particularly in undertakings, added that workers see the unions as being made up of rival and somewhat remote factions, whose leaders participate in discussions at the highest levels. The unions, which were called upon to play a major role in the economic and social life of the country as soon as they came out into the open, have not always had the time or the opportunity to consolidate the trade union structure at the intermediate level between the undertaking and the leadership in Madrid (or in the autonomous communities) and to establish the necessary links all the way to the top of the union hierarchy. The union leaders the mission encountered stressed the effort that they were now making, through meetings, publications and other means, to inform and to mobilise their members and all their sympathisers.

However, though membership is low — and the fear of a sudden change of regime and persecution of union members is also said to have a bearing on the situation — the unions have apparently aroused a great deal of interest, and an increasing number of workers now vote for the UGT or the CCOO in union elections. It is difficult to give an exact indication of the percentage of votes obtained by each confederation, as they are often the subject of controversy (this is not the case in the Basque country, where the ELA-STV, UGT and CCOO have agreed on arrangements for monitoring union elections). However, judging from the results of the 1982 elections [10] (reproduced in table 1), the UGT appears today to be the most representative union. It won approximately 36 per cent of the votes, ahead of the CCOO which received about 33 per cent; the UGT appears in particular to have had a great deal of support in small and medium-sized undertakings; the USO received 4-5 per cent of votes. The election confirms that support for the CNT has been reduced to a few minor groups of isolated militants (for instance in Andalusia, Barcelona, Castellón, Valencia, Alava). The regional unions, the ELA-STV in the Basque country (the first union of the region with approximately 30 per cent of the votes) and the

Table 1.   Trade union elections between 15 March and 31 December 1982

Trade union	No. of representatives elected	Percentage	
		State	Autonomous communities
UGT	51 672	36.71	
CCOO	47 016	33.40	
USO	6 527	4.64	
INTG	1 651	1.17	18.94
ELA-STV	4 642	3.30	30.24
Unaffiliated	17 024	12.09	
Miscellaneous	12 238	8.69	
Total	140 770	100.00	
No. entitled to vote	2 463 518		
Votes cast	1 950 335	79.17	

Source. Resolutions of the National Mediation, Arbitration and Conciliation Institute of 2 April 1981 and 10 March 1983.

INTG in Galicia (which, while not the largest, won more than the 15 per cent of votes required to be considered representative in this area of the country), also did very well.

In the public sector, the union organisations referred to above obtained about 70 per cent of votes; the unions which claim to be independent (and which the others sometimes consider to be the heirs to the vertical unions of the preceding period) obtained only the remaining 30 per cent.

Generally speaking, the large trade union confederations are particularly strong in such sectors as the metal trades, chemicals, construction and textiles. The same is true of many other industrialised countries. However, the mission was told that, largely as a result of the crisis, the occupational federations are tending to decline relative to the services sector, especially education. Though well represented in the highly industrialised regions, they are much less so in the agricultural areas.

Internal organisation and international affiliation

With a few exceptions such as airline pilots, workers join unions according to branch of activity rather than occupation, a tendency found in many countries nowadays.

The by-laws of the various trade union confederations obviously contain a large number of provisions dealing with their internal structure. The UGT, which is affiliated to the ICFTU and the European Trade Union Confederation (ETUC), has a very simple structure. The local (or provincial or district) union organised by branch of industry is the basic unit; it is composed of workers from various union sections at the level of the undertaking. The unions then combine to form occupational federations. The UGT is composed of these federations

31

together with the territorial unions (at the local, district, provincial, regional and autonomous community levels), which co-ordinate the activities of organisations in a given geographical area, and the so-called "external" unions of Spanish emigrant workers.

The UGT's supreme body is the Congress, which is normally held every three years. Between sessions, the confederation is represented by the Confederal Committee. The Executive Committee, elected by the Congress, is the permanent governing body.

The two Committees have certain co-ordinating powers which have naturally been enhanced by the trend towards consultation and negotiation at the national level. Officials of the confederation are, however, accompanied in such discussions by the leaders of the main occupational federations (all of which, together with the territorial unions, are represented on the Confederal Committee). The by-laws also include provisions concerning the rights of organisations at the lower levels. These organisations may, for example, call a work stoppage on their own initiative; before a strike is called, the executive committee of the occupational federation in question — and not, it should be stressed, the UGT's central bodies — may send a delegation to the spot in order to settle the dispute, but only with the agreement of the organisation directly concerned.[11]

The CCOO is not a member of any international confederation. The smallest cell of the organisation is the union section in the undertaking, and senior CCOO officials stated that they were concerned that workers should participate actively in them. Sections are grouped together in territorial *centrales* or congresses (confederations in the autonomous communities and regional unions) and occupational federations, which together make up the national Confederation.

The CCOO's by-laws would seem to provide for a more centralised structure. Thus, the administrative autonomy of the occupational federations and territorial congresses is subject to agreements adopted by the Confederation's central bodies;[12] similarly, in the event of a breach of the by-laws or financial policy, or a violation of the union policy adopted by the Congress and the Confederal Council, or of the Confederation's programme and principles, the highest union body may take disciplinary measures.[13] In the circumstances, the mission asked the Confederation's officials whether it applied the principle of "democratic centralism". They replied that the Confederation had adopted neither this concept nor the monolithic system that it implied but that a decision, once taken, was binding upon the organisation's lower bodies.

The representative and executive bodies of the Workers' Committees are the Congress, the Confederal Council which acts on behalf of the Congress between sessions, the Executive Committee (the number of whose members is determined by the Congress) and the secretariat.

A particularity of the ELA-STV is that it is a member of both the ICFTU and the World Confederation of Labour (WCL). Its leaders explained this curious fact by invoking historical reasons and recalled that both international confederations provided moral support and financial assistance during the period when the ELA-STV had gone underground; participation in the ICFTU is greater, through the international trade secretariats. The ELA-STV is also a member of the ETUC.

The structure of the Basque trade union is likewise organised on both a territorial and occupational basis. Its administrative bodies consist of a Congress, which is the plenary assembly of representatives of member associations, a National Committee elected by the Congress and an Executive Committee whose members are selected by the National Committee. In addition, the Confederation possesses a National Council (composed of representatives of occupational federations, inter-occupational unions and members of the National Committee), which is an intermediate body between the Congress and the National Committee.

The INTG in Galicia has established ties with the General Confederation of Portuguese Workers-National Inter-Union Organisation; moreover, the INTG's leaders stated that they endorse the line taken by the World Federation of Trade Unions (WFTU), of which their Confederation is, however, not yet a member. The CSTC, in Catalonia, is a member of the WCL. The USO is also affiliated to the WCL.

The right to establish employers' and workers' organisations, and their dissolution

Less than ten years ago, Spain was living under a regime of corporative and compulsory trade unionism. Since that time, a large number of Acts, legislative decrees and other provisions have gradually — as the process of transition had to be safeguarded — established a new system of industrial relations based on the principle of freedom to organise within an employers' association or trade union — a development which was institutionalised by the 1978 Constitution.

However, these developments inevitably gave rise, from the legal and other standpoints, to doubts and hesitations, particularly as many texts were regarded from the outset as provisional. Relevant theoretical works emphasised these uncertainties and the courts (in particular the Central Labour Court, and even the Constitutional Court) reached decisions regarding certain questions but did not have an opportunity to do so in the case of others. New laws, including those on freedom of association and on strikes, were being drafted at the time of the mission's visit. The legal framework for relations between managers of undertakings, organised labour and the public authorities is anything but settled in present-day Spain, even though certain essential characteristics may be described.

The right to form an association

The freedom to establish an employers' association or a trade union is founded, legally speaking, on several articles of the Constitution, in particular article 7 (establishment and activities of workers' and employers' organisations), article 22 (right of association) and article 28 (freedom of association). The guarantees of this freedom, laid down in general terms in these articles, are supplemented by the provisions of several legislative texts, especially Act No. 19 of 1 April 1977 to regulate the rights to associate in trade unions and Act No. 8 of 10 March 1980 to promulgate a Workers' Charter. Further texts establish appropriate judicial safeguards.

An employers' or workers' organisation may be established without prior authorisation. In order to acquire legal personality, it must merely deposit a copy of its by-laws, in Madrid or in the autonomous communities, with the IMAC.[14] The officials of this institution explained that it is because of the Institute's autonomous nature that the task was assigned to it rather than to a ministerial department. Trade unions of public servants are, however, still required to deposit their by-laws with the General Directorate of the Public Service,[15] at least until the adoption of the planned Bill concerning freedom of association. The mission was informed that it was not part of the functions of the IMAC to approve trade union by-laws but that the Institute naturally sometimes gave technical advice (such as specifying a quorum that had not been defined) or pointed out major defects to the parties concerned. If the new Bill on freedom of association is adopted, the Institute will be authorised to refuse the deposit of by-laws within a period of ten days if they fail to comply with the prescribed (formal) conditions. In the event of infringement of the law and if the breach is not corrected, the Institute informs the Public Ministry; the mission was assured that this situation does not arise in practice.

Trade union associations acquire legal personality 20 days after the by-laws have been deposited. This period is to allow the public authorities or persons concerned the possibility of requesting the courts to declare the association illegal since, as in the case of individuals and societies, workers' and employers' organisations obviously must comply with legal provisions; they may be called upon, in accordance with regulations under the civil code, to pledge their property against any prejudice that may have been caused by them.[16]

The Spanish Constitution recognises the right of everyone to join a trade union, without any form of distinction as to race, sex, or political or religious convictions. The new Bill stipulates that self-employed workers (provided that they have no worker in their service), and unemployed and retired persons may join established trade unions; however, they are not entitled to establish their own unions. It should be noted that both the CCOO and the UGT have their own federation for retired persons. Current legislation, as well as that under preparation, makes no distinction with regard to foreign workers who, though not very numerous, are to be found in the country, especially in Catalonia. When asked whether foreign workers' rights, except in the case of a few privileged nationalities (of Latin America in particular), were not subject to the principle of reciprocity in accordance with earlier legislation, the representatives of the Catalan Government explained — and this was confirmed by the unions — that such restrictions did not affect the right to become a member of a trade union organisation or to be elected to a post within one, but that foreign workers were barred from election to workers' independent representative bodies, staff delegations and works committees.[17]

Management staff may join the same union as other workers but rarely do so. Some have tried to form a union of their own, the recently founded Spanish Confederation of Professional and Management Workers' Organisations, and to conclude separate collective agreements. The question was in fact raised at the June 1983 Congress of the UGT whether a special union of technical and management staff should be established within the Confederation. Though a motion to this effect was not adopted, the matter is not closed.

There are, however, certain constitutional restrictions [18] regarding specific occupations. Members of the armed forces, the *guardia civil* and the national police [19] may not join unions. On the other hand, members of security services (criminal investigation police, prison officers, etc.) may establish their own associations for the defence and promotion of their interests; such associations must remain totally independent and may not, for instance, be federated with other union organisations. It should be recalled in this connection that, in accordance with ILO Convention No. 87, national legislation determines the extent to which the guarantees provided for in that instrument apply to the armed forces and to the police.

In addition, judges, magistrates (and public prosecutors) are permitted to establish only independent occupational groups. Other public servants are allowed to join unions,[20] subject only to certain specific rules and restrictions, in particular as regards collective bargaining and strikes.

Freedom of association also implies the right to choose one trade union rather than another. The existence of trade union pluralism is a fact in Spain. Moreover, the Constitution guarantees the right not to be a member of any union, which precludes the possibility for employers and employers' and workers' organisations to reach agreement on certain "union security" arrangements, such as practices or clauses of collective agreements which make the hiring or continued employment of a worker conditional upon his belonging to a particular union.[21] Other practices, on the other hand, such as the automatic deduction of union dues from wages by the employer, for payment to the union concerned (the "check-off" system), though not very widespread, do exist, particularly in large undertakings.

Solidarity contributions

It was obviously a more delicate task to assess the validity of clauses or practices which, as in the case of solidarity contributions, do not compel the worker to join a union but require him to pay a "negotiation fee", because he benefits from the collective agreement concluded by it. As will be seen, collective agreements normally apply to all workers covered, whether or not they are union members or members of the negotiating union, and even though they have not participated in the joint effort and, specifically, have not paid their union dues.

The competent bodies of the ILO, in particular the Committee of Experts on the Application of Conventions and Recommendations and the Committee on Freedom of Association, concluded from the debates which preceded the adoption of Conventions Nos. 87 and 98 that the instruments could not be interpreted as authorising or prohibiting union security arrangements freely agreed upon by the parties concerned. They added that the position is different when national legislation is not limited to authorising (or prohibiting) a system of union security, but imposes it. In such circumstances, it is appropriate to examine each situation in the light of the principles of freedom of association and to verify whether, in particular, the situation is not incompatible with the right of workers to establish and join organisations of their own choosing.[22]

The Committee on Freedom of Association dealt more specifically with cases where the law made provision for the collection of a solidarity contribution.[23] It considered that such provisions were not in contradiction with the exercise of trade union rights, at least to the extent that the contribution appeared to be of a reasonable amount.

The Central Labour Court in Spain has been called upon to assess the validity of clauses in collective agreements providing for solidarity contributions. In the particular cases submitted to it, which need not be considered in detail, it deemed such contributions to be illegal. The debate has now been reopened as the new Bill on freedom of association explicitly permits collective agreements to contain such clauses, provided that individual workers may give notice in writing of their refusal to pay the contribution.

Certainly the collection of a "negotiation fee" provides the beneficiary unions with income which is especially valuable because their financial situation is, we have seen, generally precarious. Certain union circles have, however, raised a number of objections to the practice.

The first objection has been raised by the new Bill, inasmuch as it recognises the right of the individual worker not to pay, if he makes a formal request to that effect. The second objection comes from the minority unions, such as the USO, as the arrangement obviously favours the more powerful unions, those that are able to sign the largest number of collective agreements. The problem is thus just one aspect of the broader issue of the advantages that may be reserved for certain unions because they are more representative. This will be discussed in the following chapter.

Finally, union leaders expressed the fear that, if the practice of solidarity contributions is generalised, the unions may gradually lose all dynamism and vitality and thus ultimately be weakened. It could also have a negative impact on the rates of membership, which is already excessively low. They added that the possibility of collecting a negotiation fee may also encourage unions to conclude agreements alone — especially, perhaps, if another worker's organisation has already done so — in order to benefit from this source of revenue. Lastly, it was pointed out that the new Bill lays down neither minimum nor maximum amounts for the contribution, and that this could lead to abuse.

It is obviously difficult to assess the validity of the objections and the extent of the dangers referred to. The answer rests ultimately with each workers' organisation — and the employers' associations — since, though the Bill authorises these arrangements, it does not make them mandatory. The UGT has come out clearly in favour of the arrangement, the ELA-STV, INTG and USO have firmly opposed it and, at the time of the mission's visit, the CCOO, while expressing reservations, had not officially rejected it.

Anti-union practices

The right of workers to join union organisations of their own choosing presupposes the right not to be subjected to reprisals on account of such membership and therefore to be protected against anti-union practices, particularly on the part of the employer: dismissal, refusal to hire, suspension, transfer, delayed promotion and so on, on grounds of union membership or activities. ILO Convention No. 98 provides expressly that workers are to enjoy adequate protection against acts of anti-union discrimination liable to infringe their right of freedom of association at the time of hiring and throughout the employment relationship. Convention No. 135 and Recommendation No. 143 deal specifically with the protection of workers' representatives in the undertaking who, by the nature of their functions, are more exposed than others to discriminatory action.

Spanish legislation contains a very large number of provisions in this field. Furthermore, the inter-confederation framework agreement concluded in January 1980 between the CEOE and the UGT — to which the USO later became a party — recognised the fact of trade union presence in undertakings, and its relevant provisions have been included in subsequent agreements. The essential point is that, under the Act of 1977 on right of association,[24] workers and employers enjoy legal protection against any act of anti-union discrimination in respect of their employment or activities. Moreover, Act No. 62 of 26 December 1978 institutes a special, accelerated procedure in the ordinary courts for protecting fundamental rights, including freedom of association;[25] the procedure appears, however, to be little used. The Act promulgating a Workers' Charter contains several provisions affording protection[26] either to union members in general or to workers' representatives recognised as such by law. Lastly, the Penal Code provides for penalties for any person who prevents or impedes the legitimate exercise of freedom of association or in any way seriously disrupts the statutory activities of a lawful association.[27] The inter-confederation framework agreement of 1980 referred expressly to all these texts.

What is important, of course, is whether these instruments are sufficient to provide effective protection against acts of anti-union discrimination. The mission therefore often raised this question, especially with the trade unions. The union officials replied that acts of anti-union discrimination are of course committed, particularly in small undertakings, and that there are of course employers who still do not really accept the presence of unions in their factory or business. They added, however, that one could not possibly speak of a generalised problem, still less of a climate of repression. They referred to the difficulty of making sure that the relevant legislation is enforced, particularly in areas where trade unionism is not well established (as it is the strength of the workers' organisations that constitutes the best safeguard against such practices), as indicative of the anti-union nature of particular cases of dismissal.

Anti-union practices seem more widespread in Catalonia than elsewhere, according to the union leaders the mission met in Barcelona, at the headquarters of both the UGT and the CCOO. They complained of the shortcomings and slowness of judicial proceedings and of what they saw as the judges' leniency towards the anti-union aspects of certain measures. They also regretted that it was often sufficient for an employer to pay compensation to be able to dismiss freely anyone he wished.

However, it was pointed out that the current Bill on freedom of association should appreciably increase penalties for discriminatory practices. The Bill declares null and void [28] any regulations, collective agreement clauses, individual contracts or employers' decisions which contain or imply any form of discrimination in respect of employment or working conditions — whether positive or negative — based on membership (or non-membership) of a union, agreements concluded by a union or, more generally, the exercise of union activities.[29]

The mission was further informed by trade union sources that employers sometimes encouraged the creation or activities of so-called "independent" unions. Under the Act on right of association,[30] workers' and employers' organisations manage their affairs with complete autonomy and enjoy legal protection against any act of interference by each other. ILO Convention No. 98, it should be recalled, stipulates in particular that acts which are designed to promote the establishment of workers' organisations under the domination of employers or employers' organisations or to support workers' organisations by financial or other means, with the object of placing such organisations under the control of employers or employers' organisations, are deemed to constitute acts of interference. The difficulty was emphasised, in this area too, of adducing proof of anti-union practices. The Bill on freedom of association provides for better legal protection in this respect,[31] but it is obviously too early to judge its effectiveness.

Suspension and dissolution

Employers' and workers' organisations may be suspended or dissolved only by decision of a judicial authority,[32] for breaches of the law — "serious" breaches, in the Bill on freedom of association — or for reasons provided for in their rules. IMAC officials informed the mission that this may occur — although it would seem to be quite exceptional — if the founders overlook certain legal formalities at the time the association is created and if, when the matter subsequently comes to light, the association's leaders refuse to correct the situation.

Federations and confederations

The rules for trade unions apply equally to occupational federations and confederations that are freely established (which may take place before the grass-roots organisations are set up), particularly as regards the acquisition of legal personality. They may also become affiliated with international occupational confederations and, in practice, are known to have considerably availed themselves of this possibility.[33]

Notes

[1] On these various points, see ILO: *Freedom of Association* (Geneva, 1928), Vol. IV, pp. 198-199.

[2] For further details on this period, see ILO: *The labour and trade union situation in Spain* (Geneva, 1969), 431 ff.

[3] See, in particular, *Official Bulletin* (Geneva, ILO), 1958, No. 3, 27th Report of the Committee on Freedom of Association, Case No. 143, para. 187.

[4] See, for example, *Official Bulletin*, 1963, No. 2, Supplement 1, 68th Report of the Committee on Freedom of Association, Case No. 294, para. 152.

[5] See ILO: *Freedom of association and collective bargaining: General survey by the Committee of Experts on the Application of Conventions and Recommendations* (Geneva, 1973), paras. 72 and 107.

[6] Ministry of the Economy and Finance, General Directorate of Economic Policy: *La negociación colectiva en 1982: Principales características y tendencias* (Madrid, Publicaciones de la Secretaría General Técnica, 1983), p. 17.

[7] Article 38.

[8] Another organisation has identical initials: the Solidarity Movement of Agricultural Workers (SOC). Established in Andalusia, it does not appear to hold the same type of regionalist positions. It is more a social movement than a trade union in the strict sense.

[9] The mission was informed that this also applies to agricultural undertakings where, in addition, the owner sometimes fails to understand fully the desire of union leaders, coming from outside, to visit workplaces.

[10] As announced by the IMAC and published in the *Boletín Oficial del Estado*.

[11] Alternatively, the delegation merely provides guidance to the organisation: see section 40 of the by-laws.

[12] Section 14, para. 2, of the by-laws.

[13] Section 15 of the by-laws.

[14] Section 3 of the above-mentioned Act No. 19 of 1 April 1977 and Royal Decree No. 5 of 26 January 1979. See also section 4 and the final provision of the new Bill on freedom of association.

[15] Decree No. 1522 of 1977, to make provision for the exercise by public servants of the right to associate in trade unions, section 4 (1): see Seville, Departamento de derecho del trabajo: *Apuntes de derecho del trabajo* (I) (Seville, Copistería Minerva, 1983), pp. 10-35.

[16] The Bill on freedom of association provides (section 5) that the union is not responsible for the individual acts of its affiliates except when they occur in the regular exercise of representative functions or when it is proven that members are acting on behalf of the union.

[17] See Chapter 6 below.

[18] See articles 28, 103 (3) and 127 (1) of the Constitution.

[19] A Royal Decree of 3 March 1978 authorises civilian personnel in the military administration to set up separate occupational associations; however, such personnel may not join union organisations established by other workers.

[20] See Royal Decree No. 1522 of 17 June 1977 which provides for an exception in the case of senior officials appointed to political office.

[21] Article 28 (1) of the Constitution; see also article 35.

[22] See ILO: *Freedom of association: Digest of decisions of the Freedom of Association Committee of the Governing Body of the ILO* (Geneva, 2nd ed., 1976), paras. 39-42; and idem: *Freedom of association and collective bargaining: General survey by the Committee of Experts on the Application of Conventions and Recommendations* (Geneva, 1983), paras. 142-145.

[23] See *Official Bulletin*, 1973, Supplement, 138th Report of the Committee on Freedom of Association, Case No. 631, para. 34; *Official Bulletin*, 1978, No. 3, Series B, 187th Report of the Committee, Case No. 857, para. 242.

[24] Act No. 19 of 1 April 1977, section 2.

[25] In accordance with Royal Decree No. 342 of 20 February 1979 this procedure applies to matters of freedom of association.

[26] Act No. 8 of 10 March 1980; see sections 4 (2), 17, 40 (5), 51 (9), 56 (3), 57 and 68.

[27] See the Penal Code, as amended in particular by Act No. 4 of 21 May 1980 and Act No. 8 of 25 June 1983, section 172; see also sections 165 and 177*bis*.

[28] Section 12.

[29] See also section 10 (3) concerning union delegates.

[30] Act No. 19 of 1 April 1977, section 1 (3).

[31] Section 13 (2).

[32] See the Act of 1 April 1977, section 5, and the Bill on freedom of association, section 2 (2) *(c)*.

[33] Article 28 (1) of the Constitution, section 4 of Act No. 19 of 1 April 1977 and section 2 (2) *(b)* of the Bill on freedom of association; see also section 2 of Decree No. 1522 of 17 June 1977 (concerning the exercise by public servants of the right to associate in trade unions).

THE FUNCTIONING OF OCCUPATIONAL ORGANISATIONS

4

THE ADMINISTRATION OF WORKERS' AND EMPLOYERS' ORGANISATIONS

Spanish legislation leaves it to the occupational organisations to draw up their own detailed rules for their internal administration; it contains very few provisions on this matter. It should only be recalled that employers' and trade union organisations must deposit their by-laws with the IMAC so that it can verify their legality. The by-laws must contain certain particulars: [1] the name of the organisation, its registered address and territorial and occupational scope, and the authorities responsible for the representation, management and administration of the organisation. They must also contain rules on the operation of the organisation, on the procedure for elections (which must always be in accordance with democratic principles) and on the conditions and procedures for the acquisition and loss of member status; the proposed new Bill on freedom of association further stipulates that they must contain rules for amending the by-laws and on the merger or dissolution of the trade union. Clauses concerning the organisation's financial arrangements must be such as to indicate the nature, origin and purpose of the funds and the means whereby members can become acquainted with its financial situation.

Apart from these provisions, couched in very general terms, the legislation does not, for example, specify procedures for election to the management of occupational associations at the various levels.

It should nevertheless be said in passing that workers' legal representatives are entitled to certain facilities for carrying out their work (time off, distribution of documents).[2] The 1980 Inter-Confederation Framework Agreement, in addition to granting further guarantees and facilities for staff delegates and members of works committees, provided trade unions with the opportunity to carry out their activities within the undertaking (collection of trade union dues, check-off system, bulletin board, premises for trade union activities, temporary release from duties, etc.). The last Inter-Confederation Agreement, concluded on 15 February 1983, made express mention of these provisions; many other collective agreements also contain provisions on these lines. In the undertakings visited, the mission noted that these facilities really existed in practice, even though enforcing the relevant regulations is of course sometimes problematic.

The new Bill on freedom of association explicitly grants these facilities to members of works trade union sections and union representatives.[3]

Employers' and workers' associations draw up their by-laws and organise their internal affairs without interference from the government authorities. This also holds true for the management of their finances, which are not subjected to any government control whatsoever.

FINANCIAL DIFFICULTIES

All the large trade union confederations are experiencing serious financial difficulties, with the apparent exception of the ELA-STV (its strike fund was mentioned to us on more than one occasion). This is not the case for the employers' associations.

The difficulties now facing the workers' confederations can be explained by the fact that free trade unionism was only recognised fairly recently. Furthermore, it should be recalled that, at the end of the Civil War, all the assets — including premises — of some organisations such as the UGT were confiscated. Throughout the period in which they were forced to conduct their activities underground, these confederations were able to count on funds, first and foremost, because of the personal sacrifices of many militants and, secondly, on account of the functions some of them fulfilled in the corporative organisation; finally, they also received help from outside, especially from the international trade union confederations. This financial support enabled the trade union movement to reorganise itself during the political period of transition following the accession to the throne of King Juan Carlos I; as the Secretary-General of the USO, Manuel Zaguirre Cano, pointed out, this aid has not completely dried up even today.

Apart from the low membership rates, the main problem facing many trade union confederations at the moment seems to be their difficulty in collecting trade union dues. Many trade union members do not pay their contributions on a regular basis; moreover, unemployed workers, which as already noted are very numerous, may find it difficult to do so (in some organisations, their contribution is only symbolic). Although the inter-confederation agreements referred to provide for a check-off arrangement, workers are not always in favour of this system; perhaps, as the mission was told, they might be afraid of showing, both within the undertaking or outside, that they belong to a trade union which until very recently was clandestine. Furthermore, and unlike the UGT and the CCOO, the ELA-STV is opposed to this system, not, we were assured by its leaders, on principle but because of prevailing conditions in the Basque country.

Union dues are the same for all categories of workers, although some believe that it should be made proportional to the income of every individual; at the time the mission visited Spain, it ranged from 200-300 pesetas [4] per month in most of the unions to 590 pesetas for the ELA-STV. For example, UGT members paid a minimum contribution of 275 pesetas (i.e. 0.7 per cent of the minimum wage) but the occupational federations could decide upon an increase and maintain it (at that time, the contribution was about 300 pesetas); 10 per cent of the contributions was paid to the confederation and the remainder was divided up between the other levels of the trade union hierarchy.

In view of this shortage of funds, the trade union organisations have had to take out loans to be able to carry out all their activities and grant workers certain services which are traditional in Spain, such as free legal aid (which, we were told by the UGT, is very expensive), other forms of assistance, cultural and sporting activities, travel arrangements and, in the case of the UGT, participation in the management of workers' recreation centres and so on. Alongside the National Employment Agreement, signed in June 1981, they negotiated an agreement with the Government on the allocation of an overall sum of 800 million pesetas for 1982, 1983 and 1984, to come out of the national budget. These payments, made by the Government pending distribution of the assets of the former corporative organisation, were to be divided up amongst the trade union confederations considered as representative, in proportion to their degree of "representativity", calculated on the basis of trade union elections. The CEOE expressed strong reservations on this arrangement. For their part, the minority organisations (first the CNT, then the USO, when it no longer received a subsidy after the trade union elections in 1982) initiated legal proceedings to have the decision to exclude them overturned; they obtained satisfaction from the Supreme Court and, during the mission, the matter was being examined by the Constitutional Court. Other trade union confederations, such as the ELA-STV, also expressed their reservations on this method of financing trade unions, although they themselves received a subsidy. Others, for example the UGT, informed the mission that the sums received were mainly earmarked for training purposes, to which they attached particular importance.

It should be added that the governments of some autonomous communities (the Basque country, Catalonia and Galicia were mentioned) also grant subsidies of varying amounts to trade union organisations.

The debate over trade union assets

The handing over of the assets of the former corporative trade union organisation is undoubtedly one of the thorniest issues facing Spain today in the field of industrial relations. The matter has in fact been raised with the Committee on Freedom of Association of the Governing Body of the ILO.[5]

The assets are of two kinds: those confiscated from trade union organisations and some employers' associations and transferred to the corporative organisation at the end of the Civil War (which the Spanish call the "historic" assets); and the income the latter organisation received during the course of its existence, which derived especially from compulsory dues ("accumulated" assets). The distribution of the latter category of assets is obviously a particularly intricate matter, but even the return of confiscated buildings can give rise to numerous problems when they have been destroyed, rebuilt or sold, etc.

The Government has already returned some confiscated premises, which were identifiable and in a good state, to their former owners. Although the process of handing over these buildings is to continue, many complex legal situations must first be cleared up (for example, several trade union movements claim to be the successors to the former CNT).

The above-mentioned arrangements concluded between the Government and the major trade union confederations outside the framework of the 1981 National Employment Agreement also contain clauses on the transfer of the usufruct or use of some buildings which had been part of the "accumulated" assets to workers' and employers' organisations. In spite of its reservations on the arrangement as a whole, the CEOE agreed to benefit from the latter provisions. On this basis, premises were handed over to the employers' confederation — which nevertheless considered that it had not received enough — and to the UGT, CCOO, USO and INTG. The CNT, left out of the arrangement, appealed to the courts, and the Constitutional Court finally ruled that there should be no discrimination against the CNT in the distribution of these buildings. Other trade unions also complained to us that they had not received their fair share, such as the USO and the INTG, or that they had not received any at all, such as the ELA-STV.

There are three basic schools of thought on how the assets accumulated by the corporative organisation over the years should be finally distributed. Some believe that all the capital should go to the State since the institutions which made up this organisation came under public law. Others, for example the CEOE, whilst supporting the first argument, point out that if the distribution takes place it must take into account the proportion of the compulsory dues paid by the employers, i.e. 85 per cent. Finally, most of the trade union leaders — and the CCOO informed the mission that its position on the matter was almost the same as that of the UGT — believe that in one way or another the money came out of the workers' wages and that it should be returned to their organisations.

The Committee on Freedom of Association [6] has urged that there should be consultation of the representative organisations of employers and workers with a view to working out a final solution to the problem of the disposal of the assets accumulated by the former official trade union organisation. It added that such a solution should be based on the principle that assets should be used for the purpose for which they were intended and not on the exact amount of the contributions paid to the former organisation by either party. The return of the confiscated assets should be a matter of negotiation between the Government and the representatives of the occupational organisations concerned. The Committee expressed the hope that the authorities would take the necessary steps at an early date to enable a solution to be found in a spirit of co-operation amongst all the parties concerned.

Today, the principle of the distribution of these "accumulated" assets has been accepted, but the way in which it should take place has not yet been finally decided upon. The Under-Secretary of Labour and Social Security, Mr. Segismundo Crespo Valera, informed the mission that it would be carried out on the basis of an Act, which would be guided by the recommendations of the Committee on Freedom of Association; in particular, the criteria for the distribution would be based on the principle that assets should be used for the purpose for which they were intended. The necessary decisions have not yet been taken but, it goes without saying, the drafting of the Act has already given rise to all sorts of conjecture, suspicion and tension and everyone hopes that the problem will quickly be resolved.

THE ACTIVITIES OF OCCUPATIONAL ORGANISATIONS

Trade union rights and civil liberties

Trade union organisations and employers' associations can only defend their members adequately, promote their interests fully or fulfil the duties for which they were set up under a regime which guarantees fundamental human rights. This has often been stressed within the ILO, and the Committee of Experts on the Application of Conventions and Recommendations recently reiterated these principles in a general survey entitled *Freedom of association and collective bargaining*.[7]

At this point, it is also relevant to recall that the International Labour Conference, in a resolution adopted in 1970,[8] recognised that the rights conferred upon workers' and employers' organisations must be based on respect for those civil liberties which have been enunciated in particular in the Universal Declaration of Human Rights and in the International Covenant on Civil and Political Rights, and that the absence of these civil liberties removes all meaning from the concept of trade union rights. It referred especially to the freedom and security of persons (as well as freedom from arbitrary arrest and detention), freedom of opinion and expression (in particular, freedom to hold opinions without interference and to seek, receive and impart information and ideas through any media and regardless of frontiers), freedom of assembly, the right to a fair trial by an independent and impartial tribunal and the right to protection of the property of trade union organisations.

It was clearly stated by various sources, especially in trade union circles, that there were no longer any obstacles to the application of these human rights in Spain, even if sometimes, as in all countries, there might be breaches in practice. It is well known that, in the past, many allegations were brought before the Committee on Freedom of Association concerning violent clashes between policemen and strikers (clashes which had sometimes resulted in the death of workers), arrests linked to trade union activities and even ill-treatment in prison. This is no longer the case today.

The 1978 Constitution lays down many fundamental rights, such as the right to life and physical safety, the right to personal freedom and security, the inviolability of the home and secrecy of postal and other communications, protection against abuses in data processing, the right to communicate freely or receive information, freedom of opinion, right of assembly and right of association. Most of these rights are safeguarded by legal procedures providing special guarantees, as has already been mentioned.[9]

The Constitution also prohibits special or extraordinary courts [10] and sets up a Constitutional Court which may rule that part or all of an act is unconstitutional or hear individual appeals against violations of basic rights and civil liberties.[11]

As far as the Penal Code is concerned, it punishes crimes and offences against human dignity and an individual's physical safety, freedom and personal security and especially sanctions officials who attempt to hinder the exercise of established rights; it also provides for sanctions against those who prevent or try to hinder the legitimate exercise of freedom of expression, of assembly and of association.[12]

A recent Act has done away with the need to obtain prior authorisation before holding a meeting.[13] It merely stipulates that the authorities should be notified in advance if the gathering is to take place on a public thoroughfare or in the case of a demonstration; the public authorities may only ban it if they have reason to believe that it would disturb law and order and endanger individuals or property. They may also stop or break up a meeting or demonstration which is illegal under the terms of the Penal Code or which has caused disturbances of law and order. The Act stipulates that these meetings may only be organised by persons in full possession of their civil rights.

The Workers' Charter of 1980 considers freedom of association and the right of assembly as basic rights of the workers; it also contains, as will be seen later, several sections on the right of assembly in the undertaking.[14] These provisions, like those concerning staff delegates and works committees, nevertheless establish a system of representation which cannot be considered as a form of trade union action, even though it does not exclude the presence of trade unions at the level of the undertaking.

The main agents involved in trade union and labour affairs

The legal recognition of civil liberties in general and of the right to associate freely in particular and their subsequent inclusion in the Constitution itself resulted in the gradual emergence of a new system of industrial relations. (We shall return to this issue in a later chapter.) However, it was impossible to establish overnight a system of organised relations between employers and workers, based on entirely different principles from those applied previously, without proper research and discussion and without putting the new procedures to the test. Certain changes needed careful planning. It was also necessary to test some of the new arrangements, which could of course be patterned on those existing in other countries — and it is impossible to overemphasise the extremely valuable work carried out, for example, in the field of comparative law [15] — but which, above all, had to take into account the specific characteristics of present-day Spanish society.

Traces of experiments conducted from different, if not conflicting, standpoints can be found in the current institutions. These will be described in detail later, but it is important to outline some of their salient features at this point in order better to appreciate the real possibilities of action of each of the main agents.

The level of the undertaking

At the level of the undertaking, for example, the respective role of trade union representation and the independent forms of staff representation must be clarified. Act No. 8 of 10 March 1980 to promulgate a Workers' Charter lays down the rights of collective representation (staff representatives, works committees) and of assembly (staff meetings) of workers in the undertaking, but it says virtually nothing on trade union activity at this level. However, it does not exclude it either, as section 61 stipulates that these rights be exercised "without prejudice to any other forms of participation".[16] This duality of representation obviously gives rise to controversies. Certain persons, for example at the CCOO and the INTG, put forward historical reasons and principles of united action to defend the system of works committees. Similarly, CEOE leaders appeared to be somewhat in favour of this form of representation, though they pointed out that problems varied with the size of the undertaking; the larger the undertaking, the greater the role of the trade union. On the other hand, the UGT strongly advocated a redistribution of functions in favour of trade union sections and representatives.

Others interpreted these two opposing positions as being the result of different historical developments. It has already been seen that, at the time of the corporative trade union system, the CCOO had opted to put forward candidates for the official trade union elections so as to work through the existing trade union structure *(entrismo)*. This policy enabled it, once the regime changed, to gain a strong foothold in the works committees. The UGT, on the other hand, which had absolutely refused to participate in the official trade union system, had to make a major effort to become established within the undertakings — which, some believe, is why the UGT prefers trade union representation at this level as well. Nevertheless, the fact remains that these seemingly very divergent viewpoints are much less so in practice. At present, the works committee concludes collective agreements at enterprise level in the large majority of cases; however, this body is normally made up of trade unionists in practice and in the final analysis it is their organisations that negotiate through them.

The Inter-Confederation Framework Agreement of 1980, whose provisions on the subject were incorporated in the latest Inter-Confederation Agreement, contained several clauses concerning the presence, under certain conditions, of

47

trade union delegates at the workplace. The Bill at present being drafted on freedom of association will confirm this trend. It formally acknowledges the right to carry out trade union activities both within and outside the undertaking. It also authorises trade union members to set up trade union sections, to hold meetings, to collect dues and to receive and distribute trade union information within the undertaking; the most representative organisations enjoy even greater facilities. Furthermore, when there are more than 250 workers in the undertaking, workplace or institution, trade unions with a seat on the works committee (or similar bodies in state administrations) are represented by trade union representatives.[17]

This duality of representation also raises various questions. The first is whether workers' organisations may officially elect their militants to works committees or as staff representatives and therefore campaign to this effect. In fact they can: any legally constituted workers' trade union (just as an independent group of workers) may nominate candidates for election as staff representatives and members of a works committee, who are elected by all the staff.[18]

Under the terms of the Inter-Confederation Framework Agreement, trade union delegates could also attend meetings of the works committees. The Bill on freedom of association contains a similar provision.[19]

Staff representatives and works committees may, in turn, convene a workers' meeting,[20] which means that a trade union confederation can also use this procedure to assemble the staff. According to the Inter-Confederation Framework Agreement and other collective agreements, workers belonging to a trade union may also meet among themselves outside normal working hours and without disrupting the normal course of work within the undertaking. The Bill on freedom of association reaffirms this possibility.[21]

The union leaders whom the mission met, especially in the undertakings, admitted that participation was not always very high either at staff meetings or at trade union meetings but varied according to the time at which the meeting was held and the subject under discussion (there could, for example, be a massive attendance to discuss a draft collective agreement). The mission was also informed that trade union representatives within the undertaking were obviously accountable for their activities to the trade union meetings, which could dismiss them.

The macro-economic level

At the macro-economic level, the role of each of the parties to joint discussions of economic and social issues has also varied, as will be seen in detail later.

At this point, it should be mentioned that the CEOE, like the UGT, reacted sharply in October 1977 to the so-called "Moncloa Pacts" signed by the Government and the main parties represented in Parliament: the two organisations complained at having been left out of the discussions on the major options concerning financial, economic and social policy.

After 1979 these two organisations, as well as the USO in 1980 and the Workers' Committees after 1981, concluded a series of inter-confederation agreements which are discussed in the following chapter and which were geared especially to laying the foundations for relations between parties. One of these, the National Employment Agreement of 9 June 1981, was also signed by the Government. Some observers, especially in employers' circles, stressed that the fact that the Government had actually been a party to it, and was no longer confined to the role of mediator or even initiator of the agreement, had complicated rather than facilitated its implementation. As a result, the employers' and trade union organisations, as well apparently as the main political parties, were further strengthened in their resolve to reduce the State's role in the determination of employment conditions. No government representatives were present at the signing of the Inter-Confederation Agreement between the CEOE, UGT and CCOO in 1983. The mission was assured in fact that the Government certainly wanted to help the bargaining parties, provide them with the necessary information and, if need be, advise them but did not wish to intervene directly. The employers' and trade union confederations, especially the CEOE, also stated that they wanted to be independent from the State in their bargaining, even if this meant that no agreement was finally reached, as was the case at the beginning of 1984. All these questions will be examined in detail in the following chapter on collective bargaining.

The mistrust with which the occupational organisations viewed each other at the beginning — fairly understandable considering that they were barely acquainted and somewhat lacking in practical experience — has therefore given way to an increasingly marked determination to negotiate solutions to the inevitable problems that arise, with due respect for the personality of each of the parties involved. As far as the Government is concerned, it has sought not only to promote bargaining but also to extend social dialogue beyond the framework of collective agreements as such; for example, the legislation in the fields which concern this report was adopted only after the Government had sought, if not actually obtained, a broad consensus of the major occupational confederations.

Another aspect of the question should be mentioned at this point. Unlike the central Government, the governments of some autonomous communities — such as the Basque country and Catalonia — have been taking a more active part in the development of social dialogue within their regions. They have set up institutions (such as the industrial relations boards which will be discussed later), begun legislating certain issues and tried to tackle others at the level of the local community, with the encouragement of those trade unions which, like the the ELA-STV or INTG, pursue a regionalist (or "nationalist") policy. In Barcelona, the employer leaders of the FTN informed the mission that they were violently opposed to this trend; moreover, they appeared to refuse to accept any form of dialogue confined to Catalonia alone.

The international level

The occupational organisations are also extending their activities at the international level, through the international employers' and workers' confederations to which they belong or by means of bilateral meetings. They are also participating in the work of international organisations, especially the ILO. There is, however, one rather less well-known aspect of the trade unions' activity: their efforts to assist Spanish workers living abroad. It has already been noted that the UGT has "external unions" whose members work outside Spain; these workers are full members of the confederation and send representatives to its congresses. As far as the workers' committees are concerned, the CCOO allows Spanish emigrant workers to take out a membership card. The UGT officials in Seville (a region with a high level of emigration) mentioned the contacts the confederation was trying to establish with the trade unions and governments in the host countries to ensure better protection for these workers, and also the difficulties they were encountering. At the National Institute of Emigration, the mission was told about the historic role that the emigrant workers had played in spreading democratic ideas in their country of origin, because they had worked in countries often enjoying more freedom of association than Spain at the time.

REPRESENTATIVE ORGANISATIONS AND MINORITY ORGANISATIONS

As we have just seen, the large occupational confederations, those considered as having the largest membership, take an active part in the signing of collective agreements and, in a more general way, in economic and social consultation and negotiation. Current legislation also provides for the representation on many state bodies, as will be seen in a later chapter.

The fact that these rights have been reserved for those occupational organisations considered the most representative has inevitably upset other associations, especially trade union associations, that have been left out of the arrangement, some of which have brought complaints before the Committee on Freedom of Association of the Governing Body of the ILO.[22]

From an international viewpoint, many countries have reacted to the proliferation of trends within the trade union movement by passing legislation reserving certain rights for the organisations with the largest following among the workers, particularly as concerns negotiations with, or consultation by, employers or the public authorities. The concept of "most representative organisations" was already to be found in Part XIII of the Treaty of Versailles and is embodied today in article 3, paragraph 5, of the ILO Constitution concerning the nomination of non-governmental representatives to the International Labour Conference. Reference was also made to it during the preparatory work on the Right to Organise and Collective Bargaining Convention, 1949 (No. 98)[23] and in the Collective Bargaining Recommendation, 1981 (No. 163) and the Labour Relations (Public Service) Recommendation, 1978 (No. 159).

Both the Committee on Freedom of Association and the Committee of Experts on the Application of Conventions and Recommendations have consequently, on several occasions, accepted [24] that some sort of distinction be made between unions according to how representative they are. To avoid any abuse, they have stressed the need to ascertain that the criteria used as a basis for assessing the representative character of trade unions are objective, pre-established and conclusive — above all, normally, the number of members — and that adequate protection is granted to minority organisations to enable them to carry out and develop their trade union activities.

While a distinction between trade union organisations has therefore been accepted in principle, particularly in order to facilitate the harmonious development of industrial relations, these ILO bodies have pointed out that it is indispensable that the priority or exclusivity granted to certain organisations for the purposes of representation should not be such as to restrict substantially the activities of minority unions and thereby influence the workers in their choice of organisation. The Committee on Freedom of Association has expressed the view that the advantages accorded to certain unions should not extend beyond a priority in representation, especially for such purposes as collective bargaining or consultation by governments, or for the purpose of nominating delegates to certain bodies. It recalled these principles in certain cases concerning Spain [25] and rejected the complaints.

It has also expressed the view that occupational organisations can be representative at various levels: [26] an organisation which is in a minority position at the national and inter-occupational level but which is representative either of a branch of activity or for a particular category of workers should, in the same way as the major trends in the national movement, be able to defend adequately the specific interest of its members, negotiate their conditions of employment and conclude collective agreements. As the Committee moreover pointed out in a case concerning Spain,[27] the determination of the issues to be discussed at each level is itself a matter for collective bargaining.

In Spain the minority organisations at the national and inter-occupational level which have been left out of collective agreements as important as the National Employment Agreement, excluded from consultations with the Government and not represented in certain public bodies have naturally expressed their strong disapproval.[28] On the other hand, the two major trade union confederations at one point refused to participate in joint bargaining with other trade unions whose representativeness they questioned. The meetings with the various trade unions had to be held in separate places.

The Inter-Confederation Framework Agreement, signed on 5 January 1980, had already sought to establish criteria to determine the extent to which a trade union was representative, both for the purpose of collective bargaining, as we shall see later, and for the designation of trade union representatives within the undertakings.

The Workers' Charter established legal criteria to resolve these problems.

However, as we shall also see, there is nothing to prevent a trade union (which does not, for example, in itself represent the required majority on the bargaining committee) and an employer from concluding a collective agreement outside the legal framework; legally speaking, this agreement does not apply to all the staff but the employer can naturally extend it to everyone.

The Act of 1980 established similar criteria for the official representation of the general interests of workers or employers with the public authorities and other national services and institutions which provide for such representation.[29]

On the basis of these criteria, the UGT and the CCOO, the ELA-STV and the INTG were, at the time the mission visited Spain, considered as representative at the national level. Nevertheless, the Constitutional Court has ruled that the above-mentioned provisions do not apply to the composition of the workers' delegation at the International Labour Conference,[30] in which the INTG was not included. They do not seem to apply either to other issues such as the television broadcasting time allocated to each trade union organisation, a subject which was being much debated during the mission's stay in Madrid.

However, the privileged position of the majority organisations does not extend any further. As already seen, any legally constituted trade union may nominate candidates for election as staff representatives and members of a works committee.[31] Similarly, the courts have ruled that the subsidies or premises granted in advance of the actual distribution of trade union assets should be equally divided up between all the trade unions.

The controversy surrounding the privileges granted to majority trade unions has obviously had repercussions on the drafting of the Bill on freedom of association. The ELA-STV and the USO, in particular, strongly criticised the proposed text which, they told us, made too many concessions to the large nation-wide confederations. As far as the workers' organisations are concerned, the Bill reiterates the criteria mentioned above and supplements them. Its major innovation is that it grants representative status to trade union confederations at all levels which, at the national level, cover 10 per cent of the staff representatives and members of works committees and corresponding state administration bodies. In a non-restrictive provision section 6 stipulates, or recalls, the established rights of these organisations: to be represented in various public institutions; to bargain collectively and to participate in the determination of employment conditions in state administration; to benefit from facilities [32] to carry out trade union activities within the undertaking; to strike and use other means of action in case of dispute; to participate in the settlement of such disputes; and, finally, to nominate candidates as staff representatives, members of works committees or corresponding bodies.

Organisations set up for autonomous communities (and not belonging to a nation-wide federation) must cover at least 15 per cent of the staff delegates and members of the above-mentioned committees at this level to enjoy the same status within the autonomous community and to be represented in public institutions; furthermore, and this is new, they must include at least 1,500 of these representatives. This latter condition has been severely criticised by the ELA-STV and the USO. Their leaders told the mission that some autonomous communities did not even have that many representatives and that in others the figure represented an excessively high percentage of the total. A majority trade union in an autonomous community — which is what the ELA-STV claims to be in Navarre — might thus be excluded from any representation in the public institutions, both at the national level and at that of the autonomous community. However, any trade union which covers at least 10 per cent of the staff representatives and works committee members at the territorial level or in a particular sector is entitled at that level to all the other rights listed above. Furthermore, the disputed clause concerning the 1,500 representatives does not appear in the proposed amendments to the Workers' Charter; to be entitled to negotiate a collective agreement at the state level, a trade union set up for an autonomous community need only cover the requisite 15 per cent of the staff representatives.[33]

Notes

[1] See Royal Legislative Decree No. 873 of 22 April 1977 respecting the deposit of the by-laws of organisations established under Act No. 19 of 1 April 1977; section 3 and section 1 (4) of the aforementioned Act. See also section 4 of the new Bill on freedom of association.

[2] Act No. 8 of 10 March 1980 to promulgate a Workers' Charter, section 68.

[3] See sections 8-10 of the Bill.

[4] In December 1983, that is at the time the mission visited Spain, the average exchange rate of the peseta against the United States dollar was 1,000 pesetas to US$6.315.

[5] See Case No. 900, *Official Bulletin*, 1979, Series B, No. 2, 194th Report of the Committee on Freedom of Association, paras. 238-262, and 1980, Series B, No. 2, 202nd Report of the Committee, paras. 337-354.

[6] Case No. 900, *Official Bulletin*, op. cit.

[7] ILO: *Freedom of association and collective bargaining: General survey by the Committee of Experts on the Application of Conventions and Recommendations* (Geneva, 1983), paras. 49-75. See also idem: *Freedom of association: Digest of decisions of the Freedom of Association Committee of the Governing Body of the ILO* (Geneva, 2nd ed., 1976), paras. 369 ff. See too, for example, *Official Bulletin*, 1981, Series B, No. 2, 208th Report of the Committee on Freedom of Association, Case No. 1029, para. 429, and 1982, Series B, No. 1, 215th Report of the Committee, Cases Nos. 954, 957, 975, 978 and 1026, para. 12.

[8] Resolution concerning trade union rights and their relation to civil liberties, *Official Bulletin*, 1970, No. 3, p. 303.

[9] Act No. 62 of 26 December 1978 and Royal Decree No. 342 of 28 February 1979.

[10] Article 117.

[11] Articles 161 and 164 of the Constitution and Act No. 2 of 3 October 1979 respecting the Constitutional Court.

[12] Articles 405 ff., 480 ff., 178 ff. (especially article 195), as well as articles 165, 165*bis*, 166, 172 and 177.

[13] Act No. 9 of 15 July 1983.

[14] Section 4, paras. 1 *(b)* and *(f)*, and sections 77-81.

[15] Especially under the auspices of the Institute of Labour Studies and Social Security.

[16] During the drafting of the Bill, the term "legal workers' representatives" was preferred to "legal staff representatives", as including the various representatives of the trade unions; on this point, see F. Suarez Gonzalez: *Las nuevas relaciones laborales y la ley del estatuto de los trabajadores* (Madrid, Piramide, 1980), p. 181.

[17] Articles 2, 2 (d), 8, 9 and 10 of the Bill.

[18] See section 69, para. 2, of the above-mentioned Workers' Charter Act of 1980. A draft amendment to this Act (being prepared along with the Bill on freedom of association) consolidates the role of the trade unions: it amends section 71, para. 2, by introducing a voting list for elections to the works committee (i.e. it is only possible to vote for a list and this must bear the acronym of the trade union or group of workers concerned). A list must obtain at least 5 per cent of the votes to be represented. This draft amendment was adopted and became Act No. 32 of 2 August 1984.

[19] Section 10, para. 3.

[20] This also applies to workers representing not less than 33 per cent of the whole staff (section 77, para. 1, of the 1980 Act).

[21] Section 8, para. 1 (b).

[22] See, for example, the following cases published in the *Official Bulletin*, Series B:

— Case No. 915: 197th Report of the Committee on Freedom of Association, paras. 457-475 (1979, No. 3) and 202nd Report of the Committee, paras. 37-55 (1980, No. 2);

— Case No. 937: 197th Report, paras. 25-36 (1979, No. 3);

— Case No. 1001: 207th Report, paras. 71-79 (1981, No. 1);

— Case No. 1061: 217th Report, paras. 123-135 (1982, No. 2);

— Case No. 1039: 218th Report, paras. 32-41 (1982. No. 3).

[23] See ILO: *Industrial relations*, Report VIII (1), International Labour Conference, 31st Session, 1948, pp. 12 ff. and 39 ff.

[24] See especially, ILO: *Freedom of association: Digest of decisions* . . ., op. cit., paras. 27-38; and idem: *Freedom of association and collective bargaining* . . ., op. cit., para. 141.

[25] See especially, Case No. 1001, 207th Report of the Committee, op. cit., para. 78; Case No. 1061, 217th Report, op. cit., paras. 131-134. See also ILO: *Freedom of association: Digest of decisions* . . ., op. cit., paras. 27-38, 360 and 363.

[26] See, for example, *Official Bulletin*, 1976, Series B, No. 3, 158th Report of the Committee, Case No. 655; *Official Bulletin*, 1979, Series B, No. 3, 197th Report of the Committee, Case No. 918, paras. 155 ff.

[27] *Official Bulletin*, 1980, Series B, No. 2, 202nd Report of the Committee, Case No. 915, para. 53.

[28] In addition to the cases already quoted in the preceding notes, see *Official Bulletin*, 1982, Series B, No. 3, 218th Report of the Committee, Case No. 1039, para. 40.

[29] See additional provision 6 of Workers' Charter Act No. 8 of 10 March 1980.

[30] Judgement of 10 November 1982.

[31] Section 69, para. 2, of the above-mentioned Act of 1980.

[32] See also section 8.

[33] Amendment adopted in 1984 to section 87 of Act No. 8 of 10 March 1980. The amendments in question also slightly change the criteria determining the representativeness of the employers' organisations: the latter must represent 10 or 15 per cent (depending on the case) not only of the employers concerned but also of the workers covered by the agreement. Furthermore, additional provision 6, as amended, would declare employers' associations that are representative at the state level also representative at the level of the autonomous communities.

COLLECTIVE BARGAINING

5

BACKGROUND

In Spain, collective bargaining has undergone many trials and tribulations. Before 1938, the principle was recognised by law but, in practice, the bargaining process was subject to authority from above rather than autonomous. During the first 20 years of the Franco regime, state monopoly in the field of labour standards was the general rule, in spite of several modest attempts at autonomous bargaining at the level of the undertaking. The Collective Agreements Act of 1958 formally recognised the right to collective bargaining within a framework established by the State, which placed certain limitations on the principle of the autonomy of the parties concerned. In 1969, the ILO Study Group examined these developments in detail.[1] Some years later, the Collective Trade Union Agreements Act of 1973 introduced some improvements without, however, changing the basic structure of the system, of which the main aspects were: bargaining within a vertical trade union system; submission of the collective agreement to the public authorities for approval and ratification; and the right of the latter to issue mandatory regulations if the parties involved did not reach an agreement.

The character of collective bargaining changed after the promulgation of Royal Legislative Decree No. 17 respecting labour relations, dated 4 March 1977: this authorised freely constituted trade unions to negotiate collective agreements and acknowledged that strike action was a legitimate right of workers. Thereupon, a system of voluntary collective bargaining through workers' assemblies *(asamblearia)* developed which some of those the mission spoke to described, in its early days, as something of a "free-for-all" (others called it "chaotic" and "confused"), inasmuch as there were not really many rules to go by since, theoretically, the legal framework was the 1973 Act which was no longer applied. Later, however, the system became better organised. The 1978 "trade union elections", for instance (which, like the 1980 and 1982 elections, were actually to appoint staff representatives and members of works committees), gave a leading role as bargaining agents to the works committees, which took the place of the workers' assemblies of the immdediately preceding period, and more indirectly to the trade unions, whose popular support and representative character can be gauged from the election results. A year later, the Spanish Constitution established the right to collective bargaining (article 37.1) and the right to strike (article 28.2).

Between 1979 and 1981, several important measures contributed towards setting up the present institutional framework of collective bargaining: in July 1979 and in January 1980, the UGT and the CEOE signed the Inter-Confederation Basic Agreement and the Inter-Confederation Framework Agreement, respectively.[2] The former laid down principles for collective bargaining with a view to the adoption of appropriate legislation. The second further refined these principles and initiated a process of centralised bargaining, which continued in 1981 with the National Employment Agreement and in 1983 with the Inter-Confederation Agreement. In March 1980, the Workers' Charter added a number of substantive and formal provisions to complete this institutional framework. Finally, the judgement handed down by the Constitutional Court on 8 April 1981 upheld the principle of the independence of the parties to collective bargaining by strictly limiting the possibilities of outside intervention. The impact of this judgement is discussed in the chapter on labour disputes.

THE EXTENT OF COLLECTIVE BARGAINING

In Spain, collective bargaining is the most widely used method of fixing wages in the private and semi-public sectors. In practice, all economic sectors are covered by a collective labour agreement. The most notable exceptions are the central and local state administrations — to which we shall refer later — and some activities for which it has not been possible to conclude a collective agreement either because the parties did not succeed in reaching an agreement or because there were no social partners in a position to be acknowledged as bargaining agents.

In the latter case, it is possible in theory to extend to a group of workers included in a bargaining unit (usually provincial) those provisions contained in a similar agreement concluded in another unit (for example, an agreement for the same sector concluded in another provincial unit). This possibility, provided for in the Workers' Charter, was regulated by a Royal Decree of March 1982.[3]

During the mission, employers' organisations expressed particular concern about this decree, because they considered that such extension was contrary to the principle of the independent nature of the parties to collective bargaining and that, from the legal standpoint, it was comparable to compulsory arbitration awards *(laudos)* which had been declared unconstitutional by the Constitutional Court. The decree was examined by the ILO Committee of Experts on the Application of Conventions and Recommendations which considered that it did not appear to be contrary to the provisions of Convention No. 98, in that, as section 3 of the Royal Decree lays down, the extension of collective agreements shall take place when exceptional economic and social circumstances prevail, or when circumstances render collective bargaining exceptionally difficult because of the absence of legitimate representatives who might negotiate. In addition, the extension procedure can only be commenced at the request of one of the parties, and all those having an interest participate in the formal proceedings. However, the Committee requested the Government to supply information on the practical application of the Royal Decree in question.[4]

It should be pointed out that the extension procedure has only been used on very few occasions: up to 1983, only two collective labour agreements had been extended, one in the metal trades sector of Valladolid province (to which the metal trades agreement of the Balearic Islands was extended). The extension has even been refused on occasion, when collective bargaining has not been possible because there has been no employers' association to take part in the negotiations; this occurred in the office employees sector in the province of Seville, for which the trade union party had requested the extension of a similar collective agreement concluded for the province of Málaga.

Until 1981, collective bargaining which did not result in the signing of a collective agreement could be submitted to compulsory arbitration leading to a binding arbitration award. Although these awards were relatively rare, they were significant in so far as they applied to a considerable number of workers. The ruling of the Constitutional Court of 8 April 1981 considerably restricted the possibility of settling collective bargaining issues by means of compulsory arbitration awards. Although the latter are still possible in exceptional cases and within the limits set by the Court, arbitration today — as will be seen in Chapter 7 on labour disputes — is basically voluntary and for this reason is very little used.

The number of collective agreements included in Spain is fairly large. Table 2 gives an idea of the trend in collective bargaining over the past six years. It shows that there has been a regular increase, except in 1981 with respect to the number of workers covered and in 1983 with respect to the number of agreements. However, these downward movements do not actually reflect the real situation and can be explained by the differences in the length of validity and the renegotiations of the main agreements.

Table 2. The trend in collective bargaining, 1978-83

Year	No. of agreements concluded	No. of workers covered
1978	1 838	4 628 176
1979	2 122	4 959 579
1980	2 477	5 512 236
1981	2 607	3 879 544
1982	3 397	6 263 468
1983	3 176	5 464 740

Source. General Labour Directorate statistics.

Table 3. The breakdown of collective agreements and arbitration awards by bargaining level, 1983

Type of agreement/arbitration award	No. of agreements concluded	No. of undertakings covered	No. of workers covered
Sector-based collective agreements (national level)	50	103 115	1 454 426
Sector-based collective agreements (inter-provincial level)	16	14 340	176 697
Sector-based collective agreements (provincial level) and collective agreements at the level of the undertaking	2 769	618 122	3 269 272
Collective agreements at the level of the undertaking (inter-provincial)	301	301	548 934
Collective agreements for groups of undertakings	31	97	15 411
Provincial arbitration awards	6	24 331	42 590
Arbitration awards at the level of the undertaking (inter-provincial)	2	2	180
Sector-based arbitration awards (national level)	1	3 419	26 982
Total	3 176	763 727	5 534 492

Source. General Labour Directorate statistics.

For a more accurate idea of the current importance of collective bargaining in Spain, such bargaining needs to be analysed in the light of the various types of agreements that have been concluded. Table 3 gives the breakdown of collective bargaining during 1983, indicating the nine arbitration awards handed down during the year and the distribution of the collective agreements by bargaining level.

The above figures do not reflect the very large number of works' agreements concluded between management and staff representatives as the parties involved do not always consider it necessary to register them in accordance with the law so as to give them the status of collective labour agreements in the strict sense of the term.

Contrary to what might have been expected, collective bargaining has not done away with the former labour ordinances and regulations introduced by the Act of 16 October 1942.[5] The Workers' Charter stipulates in a transitional provision that the labour ordinances will continue to apply until they have been replaced by collective agreements. Although, in practice, almost all the sectors in which ordinances existed now have collective labour agreements, the latter rarely cover all the points that were regulated by the ordinances. For fear that some, albeit minor, aspects might be overlooked, the parties seem to have preferred not to ask for the former ordinances to be explicitly waived. Save for a very few exceptions (for example, the 1950 regulations governing workers in savings banks, which were entirely replaced by a collective labour agreement), the regulations and ordinances have not been repealed. Consequently, the ordinance is still the offical text regulating labour or the main working conditions in each sector, together with the successive amendments introduced by the collective agreements.

MAIN CHARACTERISTICS

There are a number of features that are peculiar to the Spanish system of collective bargaining. The first is the considerable autonomy enjoyed by the social partners. Established by the Constitution and reaffirmed by the Workers' Charter, this autonomy is reflected in the right of the parties to reach agreement freely (section 82.1 of the Workers' Charter), a collective agreement having such a sphere of application as the parties may determine (article 83.1). In this way, the obligation to obtain official approval from the public authorities [6] has been abolished: today, the only practical obligation of the parties towards the authorities is to submit collective agreements for registration (section 90.2).

A second feature of collective bargaining in Spain is the general validity of collective labour agreements: by law, once agreements have been signed by the occupational organisations representing the majority of undertakings and workers concerned, they are automatically binding on all the undertakings and workers covered, whether or not they are members of the afore-mentioned organisations. The case of agreements of "relative coverage" concluded by organisations that do not meet the criteria for representativeness laid down by law is discussed elsewhere in this chapter.

A third feature, which we shall examine in the following section, is the large number of bargaining levels which, however, does not prevent a fair degree of centralisation by means of "framework agreements" or, where there are none, through the influence of the national employers' and workers' confederations on their members at the sectoral and provincial level.

THE LEVEL OF COLLECTIVE BARGAINING

Under Spanish legislation collective bargaining is permitted at any level, and it does in practice take place to a greater or lesser extent at every level. However, the most common bargaining levels are the undertaking and the sector or branch of economic activity; sectoral negotiations usually take place at the provincial level, although between 50 and 60 sector-based collective agreements are concluded each year at the national level. Other bargaining levels are far less frequent: there are very few collective agreements at the level of the individual workplace, although any number of internal arrangements may be concluded at this level. Regional agreements are also unusual, except in a few cases, such as the hotel industry agreement in Catalonia. Specific collective agreements covering a particular group of workers such as airline pilots are even rarer, and in fact the trade union confederations have strong reservations about this type of bargaining which they find reminiscent of the old corporative system.

Apart from these various levels there is of course central bargaining, in the form of the framework agreements of 1979, 1980, 1981 and 1983.

Most collective agreements are made at the level of the undertaking. In 1982, out of a total of 3,397 agreements registered, 2,192 were concluded at this level. However, the largest number of undertakings and workers are covered by sector-based collective agreements of provincial scope: in 1982, 1,062 collective agreements were concluded at this level, covering 773,983 undertakings and 3,316,472 workers (whilst agreements at the level of the undertaking covered a little less than 1 million workers). In the same year, there were 54 collective agreements at the national level, covering a total of 136,087 undertakings and 1,779,688 workers. Some industries such as textiles and chemicals and some branches such as banking have collective agreements at the national level covering the largest groups of workers (400,000, 220,000 and 180,000 workers, respectively). Others, such as the metal trades, bargain at the provincial level, except for certain branches such as metal containers, which are covered by nation-wide collective agreements. The metal trades is also the sector in which collective bargaining at the level of the undertaking is most widespread, because most of the large metal engineering firms (i.e. those employing more than 300 workers) have their own collective agreement. Finally, there are two other types of agreement: sectoral and regional framework agreements. In March 1984, a sectoral framework agreement was concluded between the Board of Transport Contractors of the CEOE and the Transport Federation of the UGT, which contained guide-lines for collective bargaining at the provincial level in the road transport and urban transport sector. A regional framework agreement was also signed in 1984 covering all economic activities in the Canary Islands.

There has been a recent trend to group collective labour agreements together in order to take in increasingly large bargaining units. Already in 1980, the Inter-Confederation Framework Agreement advocated the grouping of works agreements to ensure that bargaining was at least carried out at the level of the undertaking and further stipulated that the confederations parties to the agreement should try, throughout the validity of the agreement, to promote sector-based conventions of national scope. A similar clause is contained in the Inter-Confederation Agreement of 1983. During some of the mission's talks, especially with trade union representatives, it was informed that there were still too many bargaining units and that attempts at rationalisation should continue. One of the trade union confederations (the Workers' Committees or CCOO) stressed that it was in favour of increasing the number of nation-wide collective agreements, at one extreme, and of plant-level agreements, at the other.

The possibility of negotiating at various levels obviously poses the problem of co-ordination. The Workers' Charter, the rules for central bargaining and the sector-based collective agreements themselves all contain provisions aimed at solving this problem. High-level agreements often contain directives for bargaining at a lower level, as seems to be advocated by the framework agreements. Furthermore, sector-based agreements often exclude from their sphere of application undertakings that have concluded an agreement restricted to their own workers where that agreement offers conditions that are better than, or at least similar to, those contained in the sectoral agreement.

INTER-OCCUPATIONAL BARGAINING OF NATIONAL SCOPE

National inter-occupational bargaining, or central bargaining, has to a large extent been an unexpected development in labour relations in post-Franco Spain. It is generally considered that this type of bargaining, which implies a deliberate intention to hold consultations at the highest levels and the effective control of the lower-level organisations by the higher-level bodies, is specific to systems in which labour relations are centralised, well established and sufficiently consolidated. None of these conditions seemed to be filled in Spain in 1979: the trade unions had barely emerged from their underground operations, the CEOE had only just been set up, the institutional framework of labour relations was confused, to say the least, and there was an exceptionally high number of labour disputes. Consequently, there was a climate of mutual mistrust and a tendency towards confrontation between the workers' and employers' organisations, worsened by the fact that for the first time the trade unions were able to press claims which had remained unspoken, when not actually suppressed, during long years of dictatorship. That central bargaining was even possible in the face of such handicaps is to the credit of the social partners who, in this difficult and uncertain period, not only in the field of labour but also in the economic and, above all, the political field, demonstrated an admirable clear-sightedness and sense of social responsibility.

It is therefore clearly important to look at the social and political conditions prevailing at the time the first national inter-occupational agreements were signed in July 1979 and January 1980. The first aspect to note is the relative institutional vacuum in which collective bargaining was carried out between 1977 and 1980. In theory, the legislation applicable during this period was still the 1973 Act respecting collective trade union agreements; however, this legislation did not apply to the trade unions and employers' associations existing in 1979 but to the former vertical trade union system which had already been dissolved since the end of 1977. Furthermore, the 1973 legislation had lost much of its relevance since the adoption of the 1978 Constitution, which established the principle of the independence of parties to collective bargaining. Finally, collective bargaining was so unreliable and confusing that the parties had to find a solution.

A second factor which the social partners undoubtedly took into account was the need, after the adoption of the new Constitution, to consolidate the young Spanish democracy, still vulnerable in this period of political transition following the change of regime. At the end of 1979, there was still considerable uncertainty as to the institutional future of Spain and the social partners were inevitably worried about the possible disruptive effects on the democracy of the numerous labour disputes, which had been increasing since 1976 at an alarming rate.[7] One of the major concerns of the social partners was therefore to take measures to limit the number of disputes, not only because of their direct influence on labour relations but also because of their indirect repercussions on the overall political climate. This approach was most successful: in 1980, there was a spectacular fall in labour disputes compared with the previous year, both with respect to the number of strikes and to the number of workers affected and working hours lost. The central bargaining carried out in 1980 and 1981 undoubtedly played a vital role in stabilising and "cooling down" labour relations, by establishing in advance the range within which wage increases should be negotiated. During interviews the mission had with both the public authorities and the social partners, it was stressed time and time again that the consolidation of industrial peace wrought by central bargaining had helped to strengthen democracy. Viewed from this standpoint, it can be said that the framework agreements, especially those of 1979 and 1980, had the same impact on social and labour affairs as the Moncloa Pacts had at the political level.

A third factor which helps to explain the significance of inter-occupational bargaining has to do with the need of employers' and workers' organisations to assert their role in industrial relations. During the period 1977-79, the CEOE and UGT appeared on the scene as young organisations better consolidated at the top than at the rank-and-file level (the CCOO, whose experience went back to its underground years, was more homogeneous). It was therefore in their interest to conclude framework agreements, as these enabled them to bargain at a level at which they had an organisational structure (and experienced negotiators) which they did not have at lower levels. The parties used inter-occupational bargaining as a means of preventing lower-level negotiations from getting out of hand. The framework agreeements accordingly not only established wage standards around which bargaining in 1980, 1981 and 1983 revolved but also laid down guide-lines both for the structure of collective bargaining and for negotiable issues.

THE FOUR INTER-OCCUPATIONAL AGREEMENTS

Between 1979 and 1983 there were four rounds of inter-occupational negotiations at the national level (in addition to a wage review): the Inter-Confederation Basic Agreement of 10 July 1979, the Inter-Confederation Framework Agreement of 5 January 1980, the National Employment Agreement of June 1981 and the Inter-Confederation Agreement of January 1983. The main subjects for negotiation in these agreements, as described in the previous section, were the drawing up of the "rules of the game" in industrial relations, the definition of issues suitable for collective bargaining and the fixing of wage standards. Inter-occupational bargaining also took into account other concerns, such as employment and the reform of the social security system.

Of the above-mentioned agreements, the first three differ substantially from one another both in form and in content. The Basic Agreement of 1979 was not designed to set standards. Its aim was to lay the foundations of labour reform in Spain by instituting a process of dialogue and bargaining among the occupational organisations. The Basic Agreement highlighted the principles upon which the CEOE and the UGT basically agreed: independence of the parties to collective bargaining; reduction in the number of bargaining units; official recognition of bargaining agents; rationalisation of the social security infrastructure; participation of the trade union confederations and of the CEOE in the supervision and management of the National Employment Institute; and establishment of an Economic and Social Council. Many of these principles were later taken up in the Workers' Charter.

The Inter-Confederation Framework Agreement, on the other hand, marked the beginning of standard-setting at the national level, although many of its provisions also regulate relations between the parties. Although the section of the Agreement dealing with working conditions did not actually set standards, it nevertheless constituted an "agreement on agreements [8] in so far as it defined the issues to be negotiated at lower levels. The Agreement set a range for wage increases, provided for a cut in working hours and stressed the need to devise ways and means in undertakings of raising productivity and reducing absenteeism. The Agreement also dealt with other important issues such as the recognition of basic trade union rights in the undertaking, the setting up of trade union sections (in undertakings employing more than 250 workers, when the trade union membership is higher than 15 per cent), the possible use of the check-off system and the definition of the functions of works committees.

The National Employment Agreement of 9 June 1981 is very different again, in both content and form. To begin with, and unlike the previous agreements, it was signed by the CCOO which, in 1980, had taken part in the negotiations on the Inter-Confederation Agreement but had not signed it. However, the major innovation of the National Employment Agreement was the participation of the Government alongside the other parties — the UGT, the CCOO and the CEOE. The Government made specific commitments in exchange for the wage restraint which it asked the other parties to observe.

The National Employment Agreement was concluded in a period of economic crisis, rising unemployment, inflation and low productivity — problems which, early in 1981, were at the forefront of the concerns of both the Government and the two social partners. Faced with this situation, the trade unions worked out a policy of "solidarity" between those who had a job and those who did not and, along with the employers' associations, requested the Government to introduce economic, legislative and labour reforms upon which an employment policy could be based. The National Employment Agreement therefore resembled a tripartite industrial agreement. The workers agreed to negotiate wage increases that were slightly lower than the inflation forecast for 1981 and 1982, and the CEOE promised to conclude an agreement on job creation with the National Employment Institute; meanwhile, the Government undertook to create, before the end of 1982, approximately 350,000 new jobs in order to compensate for the drop in employment forecast for this period. It also agreed to take exceptional steps to protect the unemployed, by setting up a special fund, and to promote recruitment, by cutting undertakings' contributions to the social security system. The State also acknowledged the right of the most representative trade union and employers' organisations to participate in supervising the management of a number of public and semi-public institutions, to which we shall refer later in this report. The National Employment Agreement also contained clauses concerning the review of wages in the state administration, including a provision to the effect that the granting of certain wage increases linked to productivity and rationalisation should be subject to consultation and negotiation between the public authorities and the representative trade union organisations within the administration. This provision is one of the rare legal texts which refers explicitly to collective bargaining in central state administration.

Although the objectives of the National Employment Agreement were not challenged, its implementation gave rise to a number of doubts and criticisms.[9] Various persons interviewed by the mission, among employers and trade unions and in government and academic circles, stressed that it was a political rather than a labour agreement. It should also be pointed out that the objective of maintaining employment, which is why it was signed in the first place, went unfulfilled since the working population had fallen to 7,638,500 by the end of 1982 as against 7,718,000 at the time the National Employment Agreement was concluded, according to the statistics of the National Employment Institute. On the other hand, the wage guide-lines have certainly been respected on the whole, the number of labour disputes has not risen significantly and the CEOE and trade unions have been allowed to be represented in the various institutions mentioned in the Agreement, as promised.

Thereafter, the social partners reverted to the system of bilateral negotiations focusing specifically on labour issues: in January 1983, the UGT and the CCOO, representing the trade unions, and the CEOE and its subsidiary, the CEPYME, representing the employers, signed a new Inter-Confederation Agreement along traditional collective bargaining lines: it dealt with wages, working hours, the structure of collective bargaining, trade union rights, productivity, absenteeism and occupational safety and health.

The foregoing analysis shows how central nation-wide bargaining developed in Spain. The framework agreements are not only "agreements on agreements", of a procedural nature, laying down the "rules of the game" for negotiating at lower levels: they also include basic provisions on wages and working conditions. They have thus become a hybrid instrument, partly a framework agreement as such and partly a product of collective bargaining for standard-setting purposes conducted at the national level.

COLLECTIVE BARGAINING AGENTS

Bargaining at the level of the undertaking

The official bargaining agent varies in Spain according to whether the negotiations take place at the level of the undertaking or at a higher level. In bargaining at the level of the undertaking (or at a lower level), it is the works committee or the staff representatives, as a general rule, that are responsible for negotiations. This rule is contained in the Workers' Charter which, on this point, only endorses a practice which dated back to the former regime and was reintroduced in 1978. The legislation passed during the Franco period conferred bargaining rights on the trade union representatives and on the members of works boards *(jurados de empresa)* which were to some extent the precursors of the works committees. During the period of political transition (1976-78), when there were no specific regulations on representation for collective bargaining, these functions were mainly carried out by groups of workers *(coaliciones)* backed by the workers' assemblies. However, as from 1978, following the promulgation of the December 1977 legislation, elections were held for staff representatives and members of works committees who gradually asserted their bargaining power "to the detriment of the trade unions, workers' assemblies and other institutions of direct democracy".[10]

Furthermore, the staff representatives and members of the works committee, elected in accordance with the 1977 legislation, were often the same persons who had negotiated previously in their capacity as trade union delegates or members of works boards, or else as workers' representatives appointed by their colleagues, as part of the *entrismo* strategy which, as we have seen, the CCOO employed in order to gain access to the trade union institutions of the previous regime. One could say, therefore, that by the beginning of 1980 both the bargaining unit within the undertaking and the persons who actually negotiated were officially recognised as bargaining agents, a practice which the Workers' Charter preferred to leave unchanged. Consequently, the Workers' Charter continued to confer negotiating rights upon the works committee as the unit representing all the workers. However, following an amendment proposed by the PSOE group in Parliament, the Workers' Charter does not give the works committees or the staff representatives a monopoly of representation but, under certain conditions, also recognises the negotiating legitimacy of the trade union representatives.

In the Spanish context it was felt that the decision to empower works committees and staff representatives to represent the workers for bargaining purposes offered undeniable advantages. In contrast to the system of trade union pluralism existing in the country, the works committee is a single unit, implying that its members must agree amongst themselves before submitting a joint list of grievances to the employer. It is then possible for the undertaking to engage in one round of bargaining instead of conducting parallel negotiations with various trade unions, a process which can be summarised as follows: one committee, one list of grievances, one round of negotiations, one collective agreement applicable to all workers.

Nevertheless, bargaining with the works committee has inevitably posed problems. The first is that it accentuates the works committees' ambiguous role, as the latter is both a forum of participation of co-operation in the undertaking and a grievance and bargaining body. As will be seen elsewhere, this latter function very much predominates. The second problem is that this solution has somewhat undermined the part played by the trade union in the undertaking because it deprives it of a leading role in what is really the most important trade union function. This may well be one of the reasons why the workers are fairly apathetic about joining trade unions.

A third problem, which exists much more in theory than in practice, is that of the possible "splitting up" of negotiations with the works committee. As the latter is not a trade union body, there is no reason why it should bring its claims in line with the guide-lines issued by the trade union organisations, and even less with those contained in framework agreements or arising out of other higher-level negotiations. This could lead to anarchy, with some negotiations focusing on maximum demands while others, for lack of trade union backing, produce relatively insignificant collective agreements. The major problem would be if the works committee had a majority or large number of members affiliated to a particularly militant trade union or to one which had not participated in the drawing up of the framework agreements, in which case they might submit a list of claims going far beyond the proposal outlined during bargaining at the central level.

In fact, since the trade union elections in 1982, this situation has not generally caused any problems because the two main national trade unions confederations are firmly entrenched in the works committees, which *a priori* suggests that in the majority of cases the works committees respect the guide-lines laid down at the national level. There are probably a few isolated undertakings in which this problem does exist, especially in the regions where the trade unions of the autonomous communities, which did not negotiate the guide-lines, are particularly strong.

As has already been mentioned, the law also recognises, under certain conditions, the right of trade union representatives to engage in collective bargaining at the level of the undertaking. They may bargain in two cases: when they make up the majority of the committee members and when the trade union negotiates exclusively on behalf of its members. However, these two situations are very rare in practice, if not exceptional. Almost all those interviewed by the mission pointed out that the only bargaining agent in the undertaking is the works committee and that, even when the trade union represents the majority of committee members, the latter and not the former officially negotiate. In only one case, in Catalonia, did the CCOO mention that the management of a large cleaning undertaking (FOCSA), in which there was a majority of CCOO members on the works committees, had signed a collective agreement of "relative coverage" with the trade union section of UGT. In practice the coverage of this agreement was general, by virtue of the doctrine of "tacit approval" (to which further reference is made elsewhere). The fact that, throughout the mission, very few cases of this type were cited would seem to indicate that, far from being an established practice, these are exceptions which prove the rule.

Bargaining at a higher level than the undertaking

On this point, Spanish legislation leaves no room for doubt. Only representative trade union and employers' organisations are entitled to sit at the negotiating table.[11] What, then, is meant by a "representative" trade union? What degree of representativeness must an organisation attain to take part in bargaining? What happens when a collective agreement is concluded with trade union organisations which do not meet the criteria for representation established by law?

These questions must be examined in the light of certain basic characteristics that are peculiar to the trade union situation in Spain, especially the existence of many different trade unions, the relatively low rate of trade union membership (which in no way reflects the trade unions' ability to rally support) and the very principle of trade union autonomy which implies the absence of state supervision over the internal affairs of the unions. It is for these reasons that it was not deemed appropriate to base trade union representation on the number of members, as this would not give an accurate idea of the sphere of influence of each union, which would in any case be difficult to verify. On this issue, the Workers' Charter adopted the criterion already established by the social partners in the UGT-CEOE Inter-Confederation Basic Agreement of July 1979 and stipulated that the representative character of trade unions would be determined by the election of staff representatives and members of the works committee. Consequently, the legal principle is that, in the case of collective agreements of provincial scope, bargaining rights are enjoyed by trade unions, trade union federations or confederations covering at least 10 per cent of the works committee members or staff representatives within the geographical area or field of activity to which the agreement relates. A similar principle applies to employers' organisations which are entitled to bargain when they cover 10 per cent of the employers within the sphere of application of the collective labour agreement.[12]

In most cases, this rule has been applied without causing too many problems. Occasionally, though, there have been confusing situations at times in sectors in which the work units are very small and consist perhaps of fewer than six workers; according to the law, this means that they cannot elect staff representatives and implicitly prevents union confederations from officially appointing legal representatives. However, in one such case which arose in the chemists' shops sector, it was agreed that, in the absence of the staff representatives needed for a trade union to assert its bargaining rights, the large trade union confederations might nevertheless claim to be representative inasmuch as they were recognised as being firmly established in the sector. Of course, such cases are too specific to allow one to generalise, but they do show that not only the laws and regulations but also jurisprudence and, ultimately, what could be termed "psycho-social factors" all conspire to produce solutions which facilitate rather than hamper collective bargaining.

The law applies specific criteria to determine who has the right to negotiate collective agreements at the national level. The first rule is the principle of 10 per cent: any trade union federation covering at least 10 per cent of the staff representatives or works committee members of the sector concerned throughout the country (and any employers' organisation covering at least 10 per cent of the employers in question) enjoys *ipso facto* full capacity to engage in collective bargaining. However, the law also stipulates that the capacity to bargain at the national level may be enjoyed by any trade union or employers' association set up solely for an autonomous community if, at this level, it covers at least 15 per cent of the works committee members or staff representatives in the field of activity concerned, or 15 per cent of enterprises, provided that it does not already belong to a nation-wide employers' or trade union federation or confederation. This rule, which might seem strange in so far as it enables organisations which represent only a limited percentage of workers at the national level to take part in negotiations at this level, is in line with the historical and political reasons that were explained during the parliamentary discussion on the Workers' Charter. During the discussion, the members of Parliament of the "historic communities" who introduced the appropriate amendment stressed that negotiations implicating the entire country could not be allowed to disregard facts that might be of decisive importance for a specific area, nationality or region.[13]

Pursuant to these regulations, the UGT and the CCOO, with respectively 36.71 per cent and 33.40 per cent of the seats on the staff representative bodies at the last elections, are entitled to take part in bargaining on almost all collective agreements at the provincial or national level. The ELA-STV, which in its community obtained 30.24 per cent of the seats, may also participate in bargaining not only at the provincial level but also at the national level, even though at the national level it represents only 3.30 per cent of the seats; its member federations have accordingly signed seven or eight nation-wide collective agreements. The same applies, but to a lesser extent, to the INTG which has 18.94 per cent of the seats in Galicia (but only 1.17 per cent at the national level). Although overall the USO obtained a larger number of seats than the trade unions of the autonomous communities, they represented only 4.64 per cent at the national level; as the USO is a national organisation and failed to obtain the minimum of 10 per cent, it has therefore been excluded from bargaining at the central level, as well as from almost all nation-wide negotiations by branch of occupational activity. Although, as the mission was told by its leaders, the USO has signed 673 collective agreements, most of them are works agreements or sectoral agreements at the provincial level (in the provinces and sectors in which the USO meets the 10 per cent criterion for representation).

Apart from the representation required of each organisation to be entitled to sit at the negotiating table, the legislation stipulates that the trade unions taking part in the negotiations, on the one hand, and the employers' organisations, on the other, must respectively represent at least the absolute majority of the works committee members and staff representatives or the majority of the employers covered by the agreement. In practical terms, this means that, for collective agreements to have the universal scope conferred upon them by law, they must, on the unions' side, be signed jointly by the UGT and the CCOO since in most cases neither organisation can on its own claim to represent more than 50 per cent of the works committee members and staff representatives. Under certain conditions an agreement may be signed by just one of these confederations, provided that it has the required 50 per cent representation or, failing this, that it signs jointly with another federation (i.e. the USO, INTG or ELA-STV) making up the difference.

In fact, most of the collective agreements have been signed by the UGT and the CCOO, especially during the years when these two federations concluded the framework agreements. For example, a publication issued by the UGT Metalworkers' Federation mentions that in this sector, out of a total of 50 provincial collective agreements concluded in 1983, 34 were signed jointly by the UGT and the CCOO, five were concluded by these two confederations together with the USO, three by the UGT, the CCOO and the INTG, and two by the UGT, the CCOO and the ELA-STV. In the other cases, three collective agreements were signed separately by the UGT, one separately by the CCOO and one jointly by the CCOO, the USO and the INTG.[14]

As these statistics show, a few collective agreements may be signed separately by a single trade union or employers' association with less than 50 per cent representation. From a strictly legal standpoint, this type of agreement is of "relative coverage; in other words, it only applies to members of the trade union that has signed it. However, having discussed this question not only with trade union officials and employers but also in university circles, the mission had the impression that, in practice, there is not a great deal of difference between collective agreements of "general coverage" and those of "relative coverage", at least as far as the application of standards is concerned. Although in some cases the validity or sphere of application of these agreements may have been challenged, others have had their validity confirmed, sometimes by legal decisions applying the principle of the "tacit approval" of the workers who were not members of the confederation signing the agreement, by the mere fact that they accepted the new wage scales. The mission was also told that collective agreements of "relative coverage" are nevertheless binding on all undertakings belonging to the employers' organisation which signed it.

In the latter case, it is worth considering what would happen if an agreement of this type was challenged by an employer who did not belong to the employers' organisation. On this point, the mission was told that the problem had arisen only very rarely, but there had nevertheless been some court rulings to the effect that the collective agreement concerned was not binding on the employers.

These rulings mainly concerned collective agreements signed by employers' organisations which did not represent the majority of the employers within the agreement's field of application, as required by the legislation. The mission was also told that, if this interpretation of jurisprudence became widespread, there was a serious risk that the balance of the Spanish system of collective bargaining might be upset. Although there can be no question about the weight carried by CEOE and its affiliated members or about its ability to rally support, this does not tell us to what extent the employers' organisations are fully accepted among employers on the whole, especially in view of the fact that the large majority of Spanish undertakings are small, employing fewer than six workers.[15] Although, up to now, the representative character of the CEOE and its members for collective bargaining purposes, according to the criteria of the Workers' Charter, has never seriously been challenged, there has never been any official control to ascertain whether or not the employers' organisations (especially in sectors where undertakings are very scattered) represent the majority of employers. In view of the fact that, unlike the Inter-Confederation Basic Agreement of 1979 (which stated that employers' organisations covering at least 50 per cent of their respective members enjoyed the capacity to bargain collectively), the Workers' Charter bases the concept of representativeness on the absolute number of undertakings, the question remains unsolved and could give rise to unexpected and unnecessary difficulties though nothing has happened so far to suggest that this might happen.

COLLECTIVE BARGAINING PROCEDURES

Collective bargaining procedures in Spain are an illustration in themselves of how the system of industrial relations has evolved, from the outside intervention and state control of the former regime to the independent and leading role played by the social partners today. In 1969, the report of the ILO Study Group mentioned that "collective bargaining can start only after the necessary permission has been obtained from the trade union authorities" (which, at that time, were not elected by the workers but appointed by the Government).[16] Today, either of the parties may initiate collective bargaining merely by notifying the other party,[17] and bargaining takes place without the involvement of the public authorities unless those concerned request it themselves. Far from acting as a watchdog, the law merely sets an institutional framework within which bargaining must take place. For this purpose, it establishes rules of a procedural and formal nature. The former concern the procedure the parties must follow in bargaining, the setting up of bargaining bodies and the majorities required for adopting agreements. The latter confer on collective agreements the necessary legal validity for them to apply to third parties. Agreements must be drawn up in writing and submitted to the competent labour authority for registration and publication. The law also requires that a collective agreement specify at least the following information: the identity of the contracting parties; the persons, duties, area and period of time it covers; the procedure and conditions for denouncing the agreement and the period of notice to be given for the purpose; and the appointment of a joint committee consisting of representatives of the contracting parties to consider such questions as may be assigned to it.[18]

In all cases, a bargaining committee constitutes the bargaining body. For sectoral collective bargaining at the provincial or national level, the committee must consist of representatives from the representative employers' and trade union organisations; [19] in this case, the number of persons representing each party must not exceed 15. As far as collective bargaining at the level of the undertaking is concerned, it is usually the works committee, as the sole unit representing the staff, which instructs its negotiators (a maximum of 12, according to the law) to bargain on its behalf. On the employers' side, the employer negotiates directly or through his representatives, who usually include the head of personnel and, occasionally, lawyers.

A frequent problem at the onset of the bargaining procedure is related to the preparation and approval of the workers' list of demands. In view of the multiplicity of trade unions in Spain, there is a risk that each trade union might submit its own list of demands and oppose those of the other unions. In order to settle any conflicts of this nature which might arise, the law stipulates that within each bargaining committee an agreement may be concluded if 60 per cent of each of the parties represented (employers and workers) vote in favour of it. However, in view of the relative distribution of strength among the main trade union confederations, which is obviously reflected in the composition of the bargaining committees, it seems unlikely, in most cases, that a single trade union confederation might obtain this majority. This has apparently encouraged the trade union organisations to consult each other, either at the time of drafting the list of demands or during negotiations with the employers' party. Furthermore, since for several years the two majority confederations signed framework agreements, the drafting of lists for negotiation at lower levels was made much easier in practice and only a very limited number of negotiations were held by a single trade union. The problem might become more serious in 1984 because of the lack of a framework agreement and the considerable differences between the positions of the UGT and of the CCOO. Consequently, there is reason to fear an upsurge in bargaining by a single trade union alone; the fact that some important nation-wide agreements, such as that of the chemical industry, have been concluded by the UGT alone reinforces this foreboding. It goes without saying that this could foster labour unrest although, as already seen in the section on bargaining agents, collective agreements concluded by a single trade union have caused far fewer practical problems than might have been feared.

The same more or less applies to bargaining at the level of the undertaking since, most of the time, the staff representatives and, by extension, the negotiators appointed by them, reflect the various trends within the trade union movement in proportion to the votes obtained by each of them during the corresponding elections. In such cases, the mission was told by works committee members, each trade union section often prepares a list of demands after conferring with its rank and file. If there is no consensus on a combined list, the issue may be settled by referendum or referred to the workers' assembly; works committee rules often contain provisions on this point. Furthermore, during the bargaining the workers' assembly may be consulted on the employers' proposals and may even be called upon to ratify the collective agreement concluded by its negotiators. This practice probably dates back to the "workers' assembly procedures" of the transitional period and it still survives today, although the law confers sufficient authority on the bargaining parties to conclude collective agreements.

Once the bargaining committee has been set up, the parties draw up a timetable for negotiations and, if they wish, designate a chairman. It is interesting to note how developments in Spain illustrate both the maturity collective bargaining has attained and the clear trend towards independent negotiations. During the years of transition, the parties frequently requested that their meetings be presided over by a neutral third person, often a labour court judge, a labour inspector, a university professor or other personality noted for his impartiality, to act in effect as mediator; however, this practice has declined and more and more bargaining committees now function without a chairman. In some cases where there is a particularly large number of bargaining committees, the parties appoint joint chairmen who take it in turns to conduct the discussions.

The participation of nation-wide organisations in collective bargaining at the provincial or lower level is of particular importance. On the union side, the mission was told that the national federations and, in some instances, the confederations themselves often advise the lower-level organisations and, if need be, act as mediators or even use their restraining influence when their affiliates adopt positions that make negotiations more difficult or if they put forward claims which go beyond the framework agreements or the list of demands recommended by the confederations. The same applies to the employers' organisations. For example, when the annual round of negotiations begins, the CEOE sends a circular letter to its member organisations containing instructions for collective bargaining concerning wage scales and other issues likely to be raised. Furthermore, the secretariats of the organisations provide direct advisory services. One of these, CONFEMETAL, told the mission that its 18-strong secretariat devotes about 65 per cent of its time to providing advice on labour matters (of the remaining time, 25 per cent is devoted to giving advice on economic matters and 10 per cent on tax matters); a very large part of this advice is on collective bargaining (which, in the metal trades sector, is carried out directly by the member organisations in all 50 provinces). This may partly explain the fairly high success rate of central bargaining because, unlike other countries with highly centralised labour relations systems, Spain apparently has no statutory provisions or binding regulations requiring that agreements signed by lower-level organisations be submitted for approval to the higher-level organisations. It could also explain why negotiations are relatively short; in Spain, most bargaining committees conclude collective agreements after four to six weeks of discussion and most of the collective agreements are signed during the first quarter of each year.

Finally, it should be noted that the Workers' Charter requires that both parties bargain in good faith. This principle does not seem to have been developed in Spanish law and practice. According to the law, the principle of bargaining in good faith signifies above all that negotiations be *peaceful* because, immediately after advocating this principle, the Workers' Charter states that, "where violent action is taken against either persons or property and both parties confirm its occurrence, the discussions shall be immediately suspended until such action ceases". However, the principle could also apply to other duties inherent in collective bargaining, such as the communication of information to the other party or the requirement to set up a bargaining committee without undue delay, which are also contained in the Workers' Charter. During the next few years, jurisprudence or theoreticians working on this subject in Spain, or even collective agreements, might contribute towards clarifying this obligation, although it may never be necessary to do so. Indeed, the requirement to bargain in good faith is almost always defined in negative terms, in other words as describing conduct or practices that are considered to be in bad faith. Of course, if no cases of bad faith arise — and this was the mission's general impression in Spain — there will be no opportunity to clarify what is meant by "good faith" as opposed to "bad faith".

THE CONTENT OF COLLECTIVE LABOUR AGREEMENTS

Apart from some minimum compulsory regulations of a procedural and formal nature (referred to in the section on procedures), the law grants the social partners considerable independence in determining the content of collective agreements. In the Spanish legal system, collective agreements may improve the working conditions stipulated by law — indeed, this is their aim — but, conversely, they may not lay down conditions less favourable than those legally prescribed.

Matters for negotiation and, by extension, the content of collective agreements were to quite a large extent established in advance by the framework agreements, whose provisions are reflected in one way or another in lower-level negotiations. For example, the Inter-Confederation Agreement of 1983 contains clauses pertaining to wages, productivity and absenteeism, working hours, the structure of collective bargaining, measures concerning the promotion of employment (early retirement, suppression of habitual overtime), occupational safety and health and trade union rights. As a result, the organisations parties to the Inter-Confederation Agreement have almost always negotiated these issues in the collective agreements of national and provincial scope. In 1984, when the parties failed to conclude a framework agreement, the contents of the lower-level collective agreements were basically the same as those usually discussed during the past few years.

In the course of some of the mission's interviews, mainly with professors of labour law, its members were informed that although central bargaining had had the beneficial effect of bringing some order to lower-level bargaining and of reducing the number of labour disputes, on the other hand it had taken away some of the interest and much of the content of lower-level bargaining, whose scope was decided in advance and was restricted to just a few subjects.

These criticisms seemed somewhat excessive, at least in a fairly large number of cases. Although many collective agreements confine themselves strictly to the framework agreements, others contain clauses which are not included in them and may cover a very wide range of issues. This is the case for many works agreements and for some agreements of provincial or national scope. For example, the fourth general agreement for the chemical industry (1984) includes clauses on labour organisation, recruitment of workers, occupational classification, trial periods, advancement, staffing, grading, transfers, holidays, voluntary separation, disciplinary measures, occupational safety and health, staff stores, works canteens and so on, which had never been tackled in central bargaining. In examining this agreement and other agreements, the mission had the impression that their structure and content do not differ greatly from those of similar agreements in other European countries and that, in Spain as in the latter, collective agreements at the level of the undertaking are usually more comprehensive, or perhaps more subtle, than higher-level agreements.

Even when several issues are determined in advance in the framework agreements, this does not prevent real and often tricky bargaining taking place at lower levels. Negotiation is therefore quite real, especially when nation-wide agreements are not directly applicable because their implementation has to be negotiated at lower levels. With respect to wages, for example, increases are not fixed during bargaining at the central level: it merely establishes a "range of increase" of the total payroll, leaving it up to discussions at the lower level to fix the actual rates of increase — all of which often entails complex discussions.

During the past few years, lower-level bargaining on the reduction of working hours, in accordance with the guide-lines laid down in the framework agreements, has proved particularly difficult. The practice followed in Spain has been for bargaining at the central level to establish an annual number of working hours and for the agreements at the national or provincial level to approach the issue in the light of the actual situation in each sector, region or province. On the basis of a legal working time of 2,006 hours per year in 1980, the Inter-Confederation Framework Agreement provided for a gradual reduction in working time to 1,880 hours in 1982. The Inter-Confederation Agreement of 1983 provided for a further reduction to 1,826 hours and 27 minutes of actual working time per year, corresponding to a 40-hour working week. However, the lower-level collective agreements found it difficult to keep to these guide-lines. According to an INI report, the average working time in 1982 was 1,865 hours, but with substantial variations ranging from 1,767 hours in the transport industry, at one extreme, and 1,914 hours in the aluminium sector, at the other.[20]

In the metal trades sector, a report drawn up by the UGT Metal Trades Union again reveals considerable differences between the various provincial collective agreements, though on the whole the objective of 40 hours per week had not been attained in 1983, except in some provinces and then only when the "continuous" working day was applied.[21] In many provinces, annual working time was 1,880 hours, but in some it was over 1,900 hours.[22]

In June 1983, the Government adopted an Act establishing the maximum working time as 40 hours per week and annual holidays as 30 calendar days.[23] Applying this Act to the collective agreements in force (which mostly refer to annual hours of work) raised many problems of interpretation between the trade unions and the employers' organisations; the former maintained that the new provisions automatically amended the individual labour contracts, whereas the latter were of the opinion that the collective agreements in force should be adhered to until they expired. A circular from the Minister of Labour, which apparently endorsed the employers' point of view, was described by the trade unions as "inappropriate".[24] Many disputes over interpretation were submitted to the labour courts, whose rulings were frequently contradictory. In other cases, problems of interpretation brought about direct disputes, including work stoppages, and the increase in labour disputes in 1983 compared to 1982 can be partly attributed to the problems caused by this Act. The situation did not seem to have been completely settled in 1984 because of the difference of opinion as to whether or not a 15-minute "tea break" *(bocadillo)* should be counted as working time. While the trade unions insisted that it be included, the CEOE stated in its instructions and recommendations for collective bargaining that following the successive cuts in working time between 1980 and 1984, the employer has never been more justified than now in not counting the *bocadillo* as actual working time.[25]

One last question is the duration and interpretation of collective labour agreements, which inevitably arises in collective bargaining. As regards duration, there is a tendency in Spain to separate wage clauses from the other clauses in collective agreements. The former are usually valid for one year and may be amended before the agreement expires if there is provision for wages to be reviewed in accordance with variations in the consumer price index. The other parts of the agreement are generally for a longer period, usually two or three years. As far as the interpretation and application of collective agreements is concerned, the latter almost always set up a joint committee entrusted with the "application", "interpretation" or "supervision" of the agreement, as the case may be. The role of these committees and, more specifically, the lessons to be drawn from their work will be examined in the chapter on the settlement of labour disputes.

INCOMES POLICY AND COLLECTIVE BARGAINING

In a country which experienced extensive state intervention in labour relations for many years, it is not surprising that one of the points on which collective bargaining was the most strictly controlled by the State was remuneration. The 1958 Act enabled the State to maintain this control by making it compulsory for collective agreements to be approved by the competent labour authority. The authorities could also issue "ordinances" for the various economic sectors, if the bargaining parties failed to reach an agreement, or other similar provisions known as "mandatory standards". Both the ordinances and the "mandatory standards" were important instruments of state control in collective bargaining, especially as far as wages were concerned. The 1973 Act made little progress in this respect because, although the obligation to have agreements approved was removed, it was replaced by the requirement to have them officially registered, whose effect was practically the same.

However, government control on wages seems to have been less stringent, or perhaps less efficient, than might be assumed from the relevant legal texts; in any case, how strict a control was exerted varied with the fluctuations of Spain's economic situation. Although the basic wages laid down in collective labour agreements had to conform in one way or another to the Government's directives, this was not true of the countless wage supplements under various headings. Apart from the traditional "overtime", collective agreements included all sorts of "voluntary improvements" and "bonuses and incentives". These supplements resulted in wages being so flexible that, when added up, they sometimes accounted for more than 50 per cent of the worker's total pay.[26] There is no doubt that this flexibility in wages took place at a time when Spanish industry was booming and reflected a labour market in which undertakings had to make great efforts to attract the most highly skilled workers.

At the end of the 1960s, with the first signs of severe inflation, government control on collective bargaining tightened up. A decree of 1968 ordered a temporary wage freeze. In 1969, a supervisory machinery was set up for wage negotiations in the form of an ad hoc committee on economic affairs, assisted by a subcommittee on wages composed of representatives of the administration and of the vertical trade union system. Its mandate was to propose the approval or amendment of those collective agreements which contained wage increases exceeding the limits prescribed by the Government. This system operated for several years. It would seem however that, with the exception of the 1968 freeze, "the wage controls practised before the energy crisis neither succeeded in curbing inflation nor greatly affected the flexibility in wages introduced, despite certain restrictions, by the Act of 24 April 1958".[27]

The energy crisis of 1973 and the rapid inflation that followed brought the question of government control of wage negotiations once again to the fore. A decree of November 1973 concerning temporary economic policy measures stipulated that collective labour agreements which, for 1974, provided for a wage increase in excess of the cost-of-living increase since the last wage review, could not be registered or approved. A further decree of April 1975 contained similar provisions but neither seems to have been strictly applied.

The change in the institutional framework, which began with the Royal Legislative Decree of March 1977 respecting labour relations, the Moncloa Pacts of October of the same year and the 1978 Constitution, completely changed the circumstances under which the Government's wage control machinery operated. The abolition, at first *de facto*, then *de jure*, of the need to have agreements officially registered and of the "mandatory standards" deprived the State of the legal backing which had previously enabled it to control wage negotiations. In addition, the country's economic difficulties and inflation continued and even worsened. Consequently, the State considered that it could not give up issuing wage directives for collective bargaining, even at the expense of the voluntary character of the latter. However, although these directives were mandatory in the public administration, their validity and effectiveness in the private sector seem to have been rather more doubtful.

At the end of 1977, following the Moncloa Pacts, the Government adopted Royal Legislative Decree No. 43 of 25 November 1977, which set wage increases lower than the increase in the consumer price index forecast for 1978 (26 per cent). This Decree introduced the practice of negotiating wage increases on the basis of the inflation forecast for the current year rather than past inflation, a practice which has been followed ever since. To ensure that the social partners respected the government directives, the Decree provided for penalties (loss of tax benefits) for undertakings which accepted higher wage increases. One year later, the Government adopted the same approach with Royal Legislative Decree No. 49 of 28 December 1978 on incomes policy and employment, which stipulated that the wage increase negotiated for 1979 should be between 11 and 14 per cent; once again, the wage directive was based on the inflation forecast for that year. The Decree stipulated that the actual increase would be determined in each case in accordance with the wage level of the group concerned compared with the national average, commitments as to productivity increases and the economic situation of the undertakings. The Decree also contained a saving clause, in case the inflation rate exceeded 6.5 per cent during the first six months of 1979.

These decrees on incomes policy should be examined in the light of the international labour standards. The Committee of Experts on the Application of Conventions and Recommendations pointed out that "the right to negotiate wages and conditions of employment freely with the employers and their organisations is a fundamental aspect of freedom of association" and that "the adoption of restrictive measures violates the principle whereby organisations of workers and employers have the right to organise their activity and formulate their programme of action; it is also incompatible with the principle that collective bargaining should be promoted".[28] These considerations relate to economic policy measures which may constitute actual regulation of wages in the form of provisions restricting the organisations' independence in the field of wage fixing. The Committee emphasised that —

where, for compelling reasons of national economic interest, a government considers that it would not be possible for wage rates to be fixed freely by means of collective negotiations, such a restriction should be imposed as an exceptional measure and only to the extent necessary, without exceeding a reasonable period, and it should be accompanied by adequate safeguards to protect workers' living standards.[29]

The Committee of Experts noted, in 1981, that Royal Legislative Decree No. 49 of 1978, which left in force certain provisions of Royal Legislative Decree No. 43 of 1977, ceased to have effect on 31 December 1979 and that, consequently, the restrictions placed by these Decrees on collective bargaining concerning the validity of wage clauses had ceased to apply since that date.[30]

Furthermore, these Decrees posed difficulties in the field of industrial relations because they were the outcome of discussions between the public authorities and the political parties in which the social partners had not taken part. In 1977, and even during the first half of 1978, it could be thought that the lack of consensus derived partly from the fact that trade unions were not properly organised. However, the situation was very different at the end of 1978, when the UGT and the CCOO, especially after the trade union elections, emerged as such a force that it was no longer possible to keep them in the background. The numerous disputes in 1978, which increased in 1979, marked the end of this approach to incomes policy. The change of attitude at the end of 1979 was the logical outcome of this situation; the Government no longer imposed a wage directive but "suggested" guide-lines, taking into account the inflation forecast for 1980 and leaving the final responsibility to the social partners. The result was the conclusion of the Inter-Confederation Framework Agreement in January 1980.

This Agreement was for two years. With respect to wages, the Agreement provided a reference framework for the negotiation of lower-level collective agreements. This was in the form of a "range of wage increases", from a maximum of 16 per cent to a minimum of 13 per cent. Wage increases could be reviewed if the consumer price index (excluding petroleum), established by the National Institute of Statistics as at 30 June 1980, exceeded 6.75 per cent. The agreement also contained a dispensation clause stipulating that undertakings showing an objectively and reliably established loss or deficit in 1978 and 1979 could negotiate lower wage increases.

At the beginning, it was feared that this clause would give rise to much abuse, if not actual disputes, but in practice it has only been resorted to on very rare occasions, probably because of the many formalities that the undertakings have to fulfil in order to avail themselves of the clause. Although it was maintained in the National Employment Agreement and in the Inter-Confederation Agreement, most of the undertakings which granted wage increases lower than the contractual minimum did not do so by virtue of this clause but in accordance with agreements negotiated within the framework of industrial redeployment plans drawn up in various sectors under special legislation promulgated in 1981.

In theory, the Inter-Confederation Framework Agreement responded to the need to curb inflation and to respect the independence of the parties to collective bargaining. However, it failed to answer two major questions: the first concerned its practical effectiveness as a means of supervising wage negotiations at lower levels, since Spanish legislation did confer upon it the authority to set standards and it was not clear to what extent the sectoral and provincial organisations affiliated to the CEOE and UGT were legally bound to respect the wage guide-lines contained therein; the second centred on the attitude the Workers' Committees would adopt as, although they had taken part in the negotiations, they had refused to sign the agreement as they did not agree with certain clauses.

Experience has shown that these fears were not justified. The agreement was so effective that the large majority of lower-level agreements provided for wage increases within the limits indicated in the Inter-Confederation Framework Agreement, and generally around the upper limit. On an average, increases were in the region of 15.3 per cent which, added to a number of "extra increases" under various headings, gave an average increase for 1980 of 16.2 per cent, whereas inflation was finally 15.2 per cent.

Up to 1983, negotiations at the national level were able to benefit from the experience of the Inter-Confederation Framework Agreement and followed its example, with very similar results. During this period, the authority of inter-occupational bargaining was strengthened both from the legal standpoint, thanks to the Workers' Charter which acknowledged its legal existence, and in actual practice, because the CCOO participated in bargaining at this level and signed both the National Employment Agreement in June 1981 and the Inter-Confederation Agreement of January 1983. Table 4 shows the outcome of these negotiations.

Meanwhile, the Government had been revising the minimum wage scales. The minimum inter-occupational wage is fixed each year by the Government,

Table 4. The range of wage increases, actual wage increases, "wage drift" and inflation, 1980-83

Year	Agreement and range of wage increases (percentages in brackets)	Actual increases established in agreements (1)	Average increase per worker (2)	"Wage drift" (2−1)	Rate of inflation
			(Percentages)		
1980	Inter-Confederation Framework Agreement (13-16)	15.3	16.2	0.9	15.2
1981	Revision of the Inter-Confederation Framework Agreement (11-15)	13.2	15.5	2.3	14.4
1982	National Employment Agreement (9-11)	12.0	13.9	1.9	14.0
1983	Inter-Confederation Agreement (9.5-12.5)	11.4	13.4	2.0	12.0

Source. Statistics from the Minister of Labour.

taking into account the consumer price index, national average productivity, the increase of the share of labour in the gross national product and the overall economic situation. Between 1963 and 1984, the minimum wage increased from 60 to 1,150 pesetas per day and the index from 100 to 1,916. By its very nature, the guaranteed minimum wage and especially its annual review have had a direct influence on wage structures and an indirect influence on collective bargaining and unnegotiated basic pay. Viewed in this way, the minimum wage is an integral part of incomes policy and has been used fairly efficiently to defend and improve real wages.

To complete this overall view of the situation, it should be added that in 1983, out of a total of 5,534,492 workers covered by collective agreements, more than 5 million obtained increases within the established wage bracket: 3 million obtained increases of between 11.01 per cent and 12.5 per cent (i.e. around the upper limit); 1.8 million obtained between 9.5 per cent and 11 per cent, with an average wage increase of 10.66 per cent. Five hundred and twenty-three collective agreements applicable to 374,369 workers exceeded the established range of wage increases, with an average increase of 14.79 per cent; 291 collective agreements covering 245,250 workers were below the lower limit. This confirms that the wage guide-lines contained in the Inter-Confederation Agreements have for the most part been respected.

The problem was somewhat different at the end of 1983. As the predicted rate of inflation was 8 per cent, the UGT used this figure in drawing up its list of demands whereas the CCOO put forward the figure of 10 per cent because, in its opinion, experience has shown that real inflation is higher than predicted. For its part, the Government suggested an increase of 6.5 per cent, the figure given in the General Budget Act for the public administration. At the beginning, the CEOE's position was close to that of the Government (it proposed a range of wage increases ranging from 5.5 to 7.5 per cent) but it later drew closer to that of the UGT. In order to reach an agreement, the CEOE requested that the Government finance the difference in wage costs between its own offer and the range of wage increases proposed by the UGT by making a larger contribution to private credit facilities. As they failed to reach agreement, negotiations at the central level were broken off and bargaining was taken up at the level of the sector and of the undertaking, with wide variations between the proposals and counter-proposals: between 8 and 10 per cent on the trade union side, and between 5 and 8 per cent on the employer's side (in some undertakings in the public sector, which were either in difficulty or in deficit, the counter-proposals varied between 0 and 4 per cent). As a result of this situation, assemblies were called and strikes declared in various sectors. However, by the end of February 1984, several major collective agreements had been signed. In the metal trades sector in the province of Madrid (120,000 workers), an agreement was concluded for two years establishing a wage increase of 7.5 per cent with the possibility of reviewing wages every six months, if the increase in the consumer price index during the period in question exceeded 4.25 per cent. Another important two-year agreement, that of the municipal transport undertaking of Madrid, fixed an increase of 6.5 per cent and also provided for a review of wages every six months if the consumer price index for the period under consideration exceeded 4.05 points. For the second year, this agreement provided for a wage increase equivalent to that of the consumer price index.

Notes

[1] ILO: *The labour and trade union situation in Spain* (Geneva, 1969), pp. 195-197.

[2] The Union of Workers' Trade Unions (USO) later adhered to the Inter-Confederation Framework Agreement.

[3] Decree No. 572 of 5 March 1982.

[4] ILO: *Report of the Committee of Experts on the Application of Conventions and Recommendations*, Report III (Part 4 A), International Labour Conference, 69th Session, Geneva, 1983, pp. 182-183.

[5] For further details on the origin, nature and contents of the regulations and ordinances, see ILO: *The labour and trade union situation in Spain*, op. cit., pp. 43-44.

[6] The Committee of Experts pointed out "that a system of official approval is acceptable in so far as the approval can only be refused on grounds of form and where the clauses of a collective agreement do not conform to the minimum standards set out in the labour law". See ILO: *Freedom of association and collective bargaining: General survey by the Committee of Experts on the Application of Conventions and Recommendations* (Geneva, 1983), para. 311.

[7] See Chapter 7.

[8] Miguel Rodríguez Piñero and Santiago González Ortega: "Acuerdos interprofesionales, centralización de la negociación colectiva y Ley del Estatuto de los Trabajadores", in *Revista de Política Social* (Madrid), No. 137, Jan.-Mar. 1983, pp. 347-393.

[9] For the CEOE's position, see J. Sánchez Fierro, "Los pactos sociales: El ANE como marco de referencia de la política social española", in CEOE: *Negociación colectiva en España y sistemas de conciliación y arbitraje* (Madrid, 1982), p. 48; and L. Fabián Márquez: "Balance de la negociación colectiva correspondiente a 1982. Perspectivas para 1983", ibid., p. 57. As far as the UGT's position is concerned, see UGT: *Informe de Gestión del Comité Ejecutivo Confederal de la UGT al XXXIII Congreso Confederal* (Madrid, 1983), p. 27.

[10] Carlos Palomeque López: "La negociación colectiva en España, 1978-79. De la Constitución al Estatuto de los Trabajadores", in *Revista de Política Social*, No. 135, July-Sep. 1982, p. 23.

[11] In 1983, the Constitutional Court annulled a provincial collective agreement negotiated by persons not affiliated to the trade unions (it concerned a confederation of works committees in the province of Navarre).

[12] Since the time of the mission, Act No. 32 of 2 August 1984 has modified the regulations regarding bargaining at a level higher than the undertaking. This Act recognises the capacity to negotiate at this level of the most representative trade union organisations at the level of the state (as well as of those trade union bodies affiliated, federated or confederated to these organisations in their respective sectors); these organisations do not have to prove their representative character with regard to the workforce covered by a particular collective agreement. An analogous regulation applies to bargaining which does go beyond the level of the autonomous community, with regard to the most representative trade unions at this level, and in their respective sectors, with regard to the organisations affiliated to these trade unions.

[13] A. Briones Fábrega, under the direction of Professor J. A. Sagardoy: *Debate parlamentario sobre el Estatuto de los Trabajadores (Representación colectiva, derecho de reunión y convenios colectivos)* (Madrid, Institute of Labour and Social Security Studies), p. 436.

[14] UGT-Metal: *Negociación colectiva: Estudio de la negociación de los convenios provinciales en el sector del metal, 1983* (Madrid, 1983), p. 9.

[15] On this point, one may compare the number of undertakings covered by collective bargaining (763,727 in 1983, according to table 3) and that of undertakings in which elections of

workers' representatives have been held (53,601 workplaces in 1982, as pointed out in Chapter 6, in the section on staff representatives and works committees). According to the law, the latter undertakings must employ at least six workers. It should be noted that they account for almost 50 per cent of the workers (2,670,524 workers out of a total of 5,534,492 workers covered by collective agreement) but only 7 per cent of the undertakings.

[16] ILO: *The labour and trade union situation in Spain*, op. cit., p. 199.

[17] The Workers' Charter Act stipulates that this notification must be made in writing and must contain detailed particulars of the representative status of the party initiating negotiations, the scope of the agreement and the matters to be discussed. The other party may refuse to embark on the discussions "only for reasons that have been specified by law or by agreement", or when the agreement has not yet expired. See the Workers' Charter, section 89.

[18] Workers' Charter, section 85, para. 2.

[19] For the definition of "representativeness", see above in the section on bargaining agents.

[20] Instituto Nacional de Industrias: *La negociación colectiva en 1982 del Grupo INI* (Madrid, Dec. 1982), p. 27.

[21] A "discontinuous working day" includes an uninterrupted rest period of at least one hour. If this is not the case, the day is considered an "unbroken working day", which must in any case provide for a rest period of at least 15 minutes.

[22] UGT-Metal: *Negociación colectiva . . .*, op. cit., pp. 22-24.

[23] Act No. 4 of 29 June 1983.

[24] UGT-Metal: *Negociación colectiva . . .*, op. cit., p. 96.

[25] CEOE-CEPYME: *Circular sobre la negociación colectiva en 1984. Instrucciones y recomendaciones* (Madrid, Jan. 1984), p. 16.

[26] General Directorate of Economic Policy and Forecasting, Ministry of Economy and Trade: *Un análisis estructural de los convenios colectivos: 1980-81* (Madrid, 1982), p. 18.

[27] ibid., p. 20.

[28] ILO: *Freedom of association and collective bargaining . . .*, op. cit., para. 311.

[29] ibid., para. 315.

[30] ILO: *Report of the Committee of Experts on the Application of Conventions and Recommendations*, Report III (Part 4 A), International Labour Conference, 67th Session, Geneva, 1981, p. 147.

OTHER FORMS OF WORKERS' PARTICIPATION

6

PARTICIPATION AT THE LEVEL OF THE UNDERTAKING

There is a long tradition in Spain of participation at the level of the undertaking. Under the previous regime, there was already a system of representation involving trade union representatives and joint boards or works councils *(jurado de empresa)*. The works councils, which were established by decree in 1947, were very widespread. Their essential function was to ensure collaboration between capital, technology and labour within the undertaking. They were composed of not more than ten members elected from among the technical staff, administrative staff and manual workers and were under the chairmanship of a person appointed by the board of directors.[1]

The Study Group set up by the ILO in 1969 analysed the role of the works councils in the Spanish system of industrial relations, pointing out their importance and, at the same time, some of their principal weaknesses.[2] On the one hand, the members of the works councils, together with the union representatives, were the only representatives elected by workers to have any officially recognised function, since union leaders, particularly at the highest levels, were chosen by the public authorities. On the other hand, the functions and activities of these representative bodies were confined within narrow limits on account of the authoritarian nature of the system of industrial relations, and of the political regime in general.

Staff representatives and works committees

This system was of course modified after the change of regime: the Royal Decree of 6 December 1977 made provision for elections to appoint members of the new representative staff institutions, the staff representatives and works committees, which enjoyed the same guarantees and fulfilled the same functions as the former works councils.[3] The first elections to establish these bodies were held in 1978 and for the first time freely created unions, which had been legalised in 1977, were authorised to put forward candidates. The principle of workers' participation in the undertaking was confirmed shortly afterwards by the Constitution of 1978, which provides that "the public authorities shall efficiently promote the various forms of participation within companies . . .".[4] Lastly, the Workers' Charter makes provision for participation in the undertaking as a basic right of workers [5] and lays down rules for the election of staff representatives and members of works committees, specifying their powers and duties and the guarantees applicable to them.[6]

Following the 1978 elections, others took place in 1980 and 1982. In the 1982 elections, staff representatives and members of works committees were appointed in 53,601 undertakings employing a total of 2,670,524 workers, of whom 2,463,518 were entitled to vote and 1,950,335 voted. The number of workers elected to one or other post was 140,770.[7]

Staff representatives are elected in every undertaking or workplace employing fewer than 50 and more than ten workers. (In an undertaking or workplace employing between six and ten permanent workers, a staff representative may also be elected if the majority of such workers so decide.) Staff in undertakings employing up to 30 workers elect one representative, and in those employing between 31 and 49 workers three representatives. Staff representatives are elected by free, secret and direct ballot. According to amendments to the Workers' Charter adopted in August 1984, staff representatives have the same powers as the works committees, mentioned in the following paragraph.

The works committee is a single body with collective responsibility that is set up in every undertaking or workplace employing 50 or more permanent workers. The number of members of a works committee ranges from five (in undertakings employing between 50 and 100 workers) to 21 (in those employing between 751 and 1,000 workers). In undertakings employing more than 1,000 workers, the number of members is increased by two for every 1,000 or fraction of 1,000 thereafter, subject to a maximum of 75.

The members of works committees are also elected by the workers in a direct, free and secret ballot. Every worker in an undertaking who is over 16 years of age (and with at least one month's service) is entitled to vote and every worker who has reached the age of 18 years and has served with the undertaking for at least six months is eligible to stand for election.

Any worker who fulfils these conditions may come forward as a candidate, provided that his candidature is supported by a sufficient number of workers in the same workplace. However, the majority of representatives and members of works committees are nominated by their respective unions, so that elections to representative staff bodies constitute a genuine periodic test of the representative character and following of each union. As pointed out in a previous chapter, it is these elections, and not union membership, which provide a criterion to assess the representativeness of unions for the purposes of collective bargaining. They also determine the distribution of seats among union organisations in various public or semi-public institutions in which the participation of representatives of the social partners is assured. Moreover, the elections, in which all workers and not only those who are members of a union take part, provide workers with a means of ratifying or censuring the line adopted by a union, while enabling unions to request their members to show or confirm their confidence. They are commonly referred to as "union" elections although, legally speaking, they are not. Since the first ballot in 1978, the elections have provoked so much interest and acquired such significance that they constitute an important "barometer" of industrial relations in Spain.

As seats on works committees are distributed among the various lists put forward by unions or independent candidates in proportion to the number of votes obtained in the elections by each list, the vast majority of the committees reflect Spain's multi-union system. In one undertaking visited by the mission (the SEAT company's Zona Franca factory in Barcelona), for instance, the works committee was composed of 24 members from the UGT, 19 from the CCOO, four from the General Confederation of Management Personnel, two from a USO-Independent joint list and four from an Independent list.

Staff representatives and members of works committees were, at the time of the mission, elected for a period of two years and were eligible for re-election. The amendment to the Workers' Charter approved by the Council of Ministers on 13 November 1983, and submitted to the Cortes, made provision for extending their term of office to four years.[8] The mission was informed in the course of conversations with the CCOO that it was opposed to this reform. The CCOO considers that a term of office of four years is too long, fails to take account of the great mobility of the workforce and could lead to a situation where, by the end of their term of office, many works committees would have very few members left, if any, which would make it difficult for them to function. The CCOO were also concerned at the fact that the reform is supposed to enter into force immediately, as elections are not scheduled before 1986 and the term of office of the representatives appointed at the 1982 elections, in which the UGT did particularly well, is therefore to be extended by two years. In government circles, whose analysis concurs with that of the UGT, the mission was informed that the idea of holding elections every four instead of every two years arose to resolve one of the problems posed by the present system, which is that it means that the unions wage an almost permanent election campaign, and may thus neglect other questions of importance to their members. Employers' circles stated that, if the proposed measures were adopted, the validity of the latter part of the period of office of members of works committees elected in 1982 might be contested from the legal standpoint, as clearly they were appointed for two rather than four years.

Staff representatives and members of works committees enjoy certain guarantees. The most important is that they may not be dismissed or punished, except for a serious offence,[9] while in office or during the year following the expiry of their term. They also have a prior claim to be retained in the service of the undertaking or workplace when workers' contracts of employment are suspended or terminated for technological or economic reasons. In the course of conversations with union leaders and members of works committees, the mission was informed that cases of persecution or discrimination were rather rare, although they did occur occasionally, and that they were attributable more to the attitude of a particular employer than to a concerted policy or a general mentality among employers as a whole.

The legislation also provides for certain facilities for staff representatives: in every undertaking or workplace, if circumstances permit, the employer must make available suitable premises for staff representatives or members of works committees to carry out their duties, as well as one or more notice boards. In addition, every staff representative or member of a works committee is allowed a certain number of hours of time off with pay each month. The amount of time allowed ranges from 15 hours per month in undertakings employing up to 100 workers to 40 hours in those employing 751 workers or more. In many cases, particularly in large undertakings, provision is made by collective agreement for the number of hours to which the various members of a works committee are entitled to be added together and assigned to one or more of the members of the committee, so that the persons concerned may be released from their occupational duties and devote themselves entirely to their representative activities, without loss of pay.

The law assigns various duties to the works committees. A Spanish author [10] has classified them as follows:

(a) receipt of information (on the general trend in the sector, the undertaking's production, its balance sheet and any other documents submitted for the information of the shareholders or partners, standard forms for contracts of employment, penalties imposed upon workers for very serious offences, statistics on absenteeism, industrial accidents and occupational diseases and so on);

(b) preparation of a report when the employer proposes to introduce changes in the structure of the staff involving dismissals, reductions in hours of work or transfer of plant;

(c) enforcement of provisions concerning working conditions;

(d) participation and co-operation (the works committee may take part, in the manner laid down by collective agreement, in the management of welfare schemes set up for the benefit of the workers; it may also co-operate with the management of the undertaking in maintaining or increasing productivity); and

(e) negotiation (as indicated in the preceding section, it is the works committee that almost always represents workers in collective bargaining at the level of the undertaking).

It can be seen that the functions of the works committees are both to promote participation and co-operation and to put forward claims and grievances. The mission gained the impression that the second function has very much taken precedence over the first. The role assigned by the law to the works committees regarding the conclusion of collective agreements at the level of the undertaking, together with their union composition, their "youth" (they were established only in 1978) and the fact that they were set up in a period of conflict, are probably the factors that have contributed most to the emergence of this trend. However, the first function does not at all appear to have been overlooked, judging from the activities carried out by the works committees through their various internal committees and working groups. In one steelworks visited, Altos Hornos de Vizcaya, the committees dealt with the following: supervision of the collective agreement, safety and health; promotion; remuneration and job classification; social questions; bonuses and overtime; and restructuring of the iron and steel industry. There was also a standing committee dealing, among other matters, with individual grievances. In another undertaking, the SEAT Zona Franca factory in Barcelona, the works committee had a three-member secretariat and committees on productivity, safety and health, promotion and employment, social questions, the disabled, canteens, case files and guarantees, transport and management supervision.

Participation in management

Under the previous regime, the Act of 21 July 1962 respecting the participation of workers in the management of undertakings legally established in the form of companies made provision for workers to be represented in the management bodies of such undertakings, in the proportion of one workers' representative for every six stockholders' representatives or any fraction of six in excess of three. The workers' representatives were elected by the undertaking's management bodies themselves, on the basis of a list of three candidates for each post, submitted by the works council. The 1969 Study Group, which had an opportunity to examine the running of this institution, pointed out that by 1967 a total of 644 staff representatives had been elected to the boards of 377 undertakings.[11]

The Act of 1962 was repealed by the Workers' Charter, and the mission was informed that participation in management bodies has now disappeared save in exceptional cases. Participation still exists, for instance, in certain undertakings of the autonomous community of Catalonia, such as Transportes de Barcelona and Ferrocarriles de la Generalidad, whose respective boards of directors include, out of a total of 12 members, one representative of the UGT and one from the CCOO. During a visit to the Red Nacional de Ferrocarriles Españoles, RENFE, the management pointed out that the authorities had designated one UGT and one CCOO representative to sit on the board of directors; the same applied to another national railway undertaking, Ferrocarriles de Vía Estrecha, FEVE.

At all events, it is certain that at the time of the mission there was no legal basis for workers' participation in the management of the undertaking. While it is true that the Constitution lays down that the State will encourage "the various forms of participation in companies", regulations have not yet been issued for the application of this provision. Certain trade union confederations have advocated greater participation in management, and in particular the representation of workers' organisations on the boards of public undertakings.[12]

PARTICIPATION IN PUBLIC BODIES

The spirit of consultation which was already apparent in the Moncloa Pacts of 1977 naturally led to the conviction that participation in public or semi-public economic and social institutions should be one of the features of the new political framework of the Spanish State. The Spanish Constitution of 1978 provides that "the law shall establish the forms of participation in social security and in the activities of those public bodies whose operation directly affects the quality of life or the general welfare".[13] Certain provisions adopted a little later have begun to apply this principle. In the Inter-Confederation Basic Agreement of 1979, the social partners addressed a request to this effect to the public authorities. Two years later, the National Employment Agreement expressly listed the institutions in which the State was to assure participation by the social partners: the national social security institutes,[14] the National Employment Institute, the Mediation, Arbitration and Conciliation Institute, the Social Leisure Institute and the Occupational Safety and Health Institute. The National Employment Agreement also made provision for effective participation in the Prices Board [15] and laid down that consideration should be given, "at the request of any of the signatories, to participation in other bodies responsible for union or industrial relations and social security".[16] In the following months, the State made efforts to ensure the application of the provisions of the National Employment Agreement by adopting the necessary regulations. Thus, on the workers' side, the two principal national trade union confederations and the ELA-STV and, on the employers' side, the CEOE and its affiliated organisations are represented today on the boards of these institutions. Provision is also made for participation by representatives of employers' and workers' organisations in other independent bodies, such as the Institute of Labour Studies and Social Security.

However, no national body with general responsibility for economic and social questions has yet been established. The Constitution makes provision for setting up a council to advise planning bodies, in which professional, employers' and financial organisations are to be represented.[17] On various occasions, in particular in the above-mentioned Inter-Confederation Basic Agreement, the social partners requested the Government to establish an economic and social council, that is to say a body of broader scope than that provided for under the Constitution. The mission was informed in conversations with the public authorities that the creation of an economic and social council was part of the political programme of the present Government, which intended to set up the council in the near future. Certain of the autonomous communities have the same intention, in particular the Basque country where a regional economic council is currently at the project stage.

INDUSTRIAL RELATIONS BOARDS

There is another institution that is of special interest in the context of this report: the "industrial relations boards" which had been or were being established at the time of the mission, or immediately afterwards, in some of the autonomous communities — Catalonia, the Basque country, Andalusia and Madrid — under legislation enacted by the competent authorities of the communities concerned.

The first industrial relations board (Labour Board) was set up in Catalonia in 1978. The board is a tripartite body composed of 11 workers' representatives and 11 employers' representatives (and substitutes) and six members designated by the President of the *Generalidad* of Catalonia, under the chairmanship of the Labour Counsellor. The board is an advisory body of the Labour Department of the autonomous Government, but it is also empowered to prepare and draw up proposals for voluntary agreements regarding industrial relations for submission to the social partners.

The mission met the members of the industrial relations boards of the Basque country and Andalusia. The former was created by an Act of the autonomous Parliament in September 1981. Its essential purpose is to ensure a permanent dialogue between union organisations and employers' organisations with a view to the adoption of agreements on industrial relations. It is also an advisory body of the Basque Government on matters related to the labour and social policy of the autonomous community of the Basque country with, inter alia, the following functions: the submission of proposals to the autonomous Government; the drafting of opinions; resolutions or reports on labour and social affairs; and the promotion of collective bargaining and of mediation and arbitration in the event of disputes.[18]

This board is a bipartite body composed of seven members from each of the two parties (with their substitutes). It also has a Chairman and a Secretary-General who take part in meetings but do not have the right to vote. It began operating in 1982 and has since held a large number of meetings, published technical reports at the request of the Government on various occasions and elaborated a draft procedure for the settlement of disputes for inclusion in collective agreements concluded in the Basque country.

The mission was also received in Seville by the Chairman of the Industrial Relations Board of Andalusia, Professor Miguel Rodríguez Piñero. This board, which is tripartite, was set up in June 1983 under an Act of the Parliament of Andalusia. It is stated in the preamble to the Act that the establishment of the Industrial Relations Board is in conformity with the most recent international directives concerning labour administration aimed at the promotion of "effective consultation and co-operation between public authorities and bodies and employers' and workers' organisations, as well as between such organisations" (Article 6.2 *(c)* of the Labour Administration Convention, 1978 (No. 150)). Other functions of the board are to foster collective bargaining (in a region where this has its own special characteristics), to promote a system for the settlement of conflicts of interest, to act as a forum for consultation between the social partners and to promote industrial relations training activities such as meetings and seminars.

It was in January 1984 that the industrial relations board of the autonomous community of Madrid was established. The Board is bipartite, composed of 11 representatives of each of the two parties and under the chairmanship of the Labour Counsellor of the autonomous community, the Vice-Chairman being the Director-General for Labour. Its purpose is to foster collective bargaining, promote voluntary conciliation and arbitration, prepare reports and studies, and facilitate co-operation between the authorities of the autonomous community and workers' and employers' organisations.

The mission heard very different opinions regarding these boards which, in any event, are too recent for one to pass judgement. The public authorities and certain of the social partners place great hopes in them. They are expected to provide an appropriate forum for discussing labour problems, bringing together the social partners and making useful suggestions to the local authorities. It is also hoped that they will contribute to the establishment of dispute settlement machinery, the absence of which is at present a major shortcoming of Spain's industrial relations system. There was no lack of criticism in other circles, however. For example, the boards of certain historical communities were said to favour an autonomous rather than a state framework for industrial relations, even if this meant challenging the principle of the unity of the market. There was even stronger criticism of the purely advisory character of some of the boards. Furthermore, the UGT of Catalonia stated that it is not represented on the region's Labour Board, which apparently is not in operation, and the General Confederation of Employers of Vizcaya is not represented on the Industrial Relations Board in the Basque country (despite the fact that union organisations and one other employers' organisation are represented).

Notes

[1] See section 4 of the Decree of 18 August 1947.

[2] ILO: *The labour and trade union situation in Spain* (Geneva, 1969), pp. 256-259.

[3] Joaquín Cuevas López: *Estructura y función de la representación colectiva en la empresa* (Pamplona, Editorial Aranzadi, 1982), p. 77.

[4] Spanish Constitution, article 129, para. 2.

[5] Workers' Charter, section 4 (1) *(g)*.

[6] ibid., sections 61-76.

[7] Data provided by IMAC: *Boletín Oficial del Estado*, 16 Mar. 1983.

[8] As already mentioned, this amendment was adopted by the Cortes and became Act No. 32 of 2 August 1984.

[9] In this case, the situation may be examined with the possibility of countering the allegation, and the person concerned would remain in the enterprise if the termination were considered to be baseless.

[10] Alfredo Montoya Melgar: *Derecho del trabajo* (Madrid, Editorial Tecnos, 1981), pp. 486-487.

[11] ILO: *The labour and trade union situation in Spain*, op. cit., pp. 259-261.

[12] See, for example, UGT: *Resoluciones del XXXIII Congreso Confederal* (Madrid, June 1983), pp. 41 and 51.

[13] Spanish Constitution, article 129.1.

[14] National Social Security Institute (INSS), National Health Institute (INSALUD) and National Social Services Institute (INSERSO).

[15] This participation came into effect in accordance with a Decree of March 1982.

[16] National Employment Agreement, section VI.2 *(a)*.

[17] Spanish Constitution, article 131.2.

[18] The Constitutional Court repealed certain provisions of Basque legislation relating to functions whose regulation falls within the province of state legislation: the conclusion of inter-occupational agreements on specific issues "and all other agreements with the object of developing a specific framework for industrial relations in Euskadi . . .", and the proposal of the extension of collective labour agreements (ruling of 14 June 1982). The mission was informed, however, that there was nothing to prevent members of the Board, acting in a personal capacity, from reaching informal agreements in the Board for subsequent inclusion in collective agreements concluded at the provincial or regional levels by the parties concerned, in their capacity as representatives of employers' or workers' organisations.

LABOUR DISPUTES: PEACEFUL SETTLEMENT AND DIRECT ACTION

7

Spanish law recognises the traditional distinction between individual disputes and collective disputes, and between disputes on rights and disputes of interests. The settlement of individual disputes, which always involve "rights", may be entrusted to administrative bodies or joint machinery established under collective labour agreements, but the final decision concerning such disputes is the responsibility of the judicial authorities. The same rule applies to collective disputes on rights. In the case of collective conflicts of interests, while various procedures exist to facilitate their settlement, in the vast majority of cases since the Constitutional Court's ruling of 8 April 1981 it has not been possible on the basis of any such procedures to settle a dispute of this type through a decision taken by a third party.

INDIVIDUAL DISPUTES

Labour courts

In Spain, the settlement of individual disputes is first and foremost the responsibility of the judicial authority, to which the Act respecting the procedure to be followed in labour suits assigns, "exclusively, the function of investigating disputes arising in connection with labour legislation and assuring the implementation of decisions taken in respect of them".[1] The labour court system comprises a network of courts, each with a single judge, covering the entire national territory. Appeals against decisions taken by such courts may be lodged with the Central Labour Court and, in certain cases, the Supreme Court, both of which sit in Madrid. The Central Labour Court is composed of 38 magistrates allocated to five divisions that specialise in the various branches of labour and social security legislation. The Supreme Court has a special division for labour matters. In all cases, suits brought before labour courts are legal proceedings, and the parties are frequently represented by lawyers (whose services are compulsory in the case of courts of appeal). The mission was informed that the Central Labour Court deals with 13,000-14,000 disputes per year.

The Mediation, Arbitration and Conciliation Institute (IMAC)

Established in January 1979, the Mediation, Arbitration and Conciliation Institute (IMAC) has various responsibilities with regard to both individual and collective labour relations. It is an independent administrative body attached to the Ministry of Labour, with its own budget and legal status. Its staff is provided for the most part by the Social and Vocational Services Administration (AISS), a body which, after the dissolution of the former trade union organisation, took over some of its functions. The IMAC is headed by a director and a secretary-general, both appointed by the Ministry of Labour. Its governing bodies are a Higher Council and a Standing Committee, both tripartite. The IMAC receives delegations from all the provinces and the major cities.

The Act under which the IMAC was set up made provision for the creation within the Institute of tripartite arbitration boards for labour matters, to which employers and workers might submit any individual or collective labour disputes arising between them. These boards were not, however, established. Moreover, as was pointed out to the mission by several university professors of labour law, their usefulness in individual legal disputes is debatable. In fact, as the jurisdiction of the labour judges is, as has been seen, "exclusive" and cannot therefore be shared, it would be difficult to empower the arbitration boards to reach decisions that are final. The boards could thus mean a considerable loss of time with machinery which is unnecessary and could be avoided.

The IMAC, nevertheless, plays a major role in individual conciliation. The Act under which the Institute was established lays down that no labour court may consider any labour suit before an attempt at conciliation has been made through the IMAC in the presence of a public servant holding a law degree and responsible for conciliation (with certain exceptions, in particular as regards employment injuries and social security). This regulation has its origin in a similar provision under the previous regime which provided for compulsory conciliation through the trade union organisation before judicial proceedings could be instituted. When the trade union organisation disappeared at the end of 1977, the parties concerned began to take their suits directly to the labour courts, with the result that the courts were inundated with cases that were normally settled at the conciliation stage. It therefore appeared advisable to restore a form of administrative conciliation, which was entrusted to the IMAC.

The IMAC receives about 300,000 individual complaints each year, of which it settles approximately half through conciliation, according to information received. It therefore filters cases for consideration by the labour courts, and this helps to relieve the pressure on the courts.

The mission was informed at the IMAC itself that the very high number of complaints received by the Institute does not necessarily mean that labour disputes are abundant. In a substantial number of cases, the parties concerned make use of the IMAC's services in order to obtain official recognition, through the administrative file on the matter, of previously concluded private agreements concerning termination of the employment relationship, either by mutual consent or, as is more often the case, for economic or technological reasons. It would appear that this practice has become an unofficial procedure alongside that of "regulation of employment" or "restructuring of the workforce" (a procedure which, in conformity with the law, enables undertakings to suppress jobs for economic, technological, structural or similar reasons). While undertakings which opt for this solution are compelled to pay a considerable amount of compensation (reportedly 2 million pesetas on average for each individual case), they appear to prefer it to the "official" procedure which they find slow and laborious. Official registration at the IMAC of any agreement concerning a worker's dismissal is an essential requirement for him to be registered with the public employment services and to receive unemployment insurance benefits.

Other procedures

While internal procedures for individual complaints are extremely widespread and valued in other industrialised countries, such as the United States, they do not appear to enjoy the same favour in Spain. Members of works committees pointed out on a number of occasions that such procedures do exist in a number of undertakings and that the works committees play an active role in them by representing workers or assisting them in submitting their complaints to the higher authorities. However, some doubts were also voiced as to their usefulness, and the mission was informed by trade union circles that the results were rarely satisfactory for the worker as, in the event of disagreement, the undertaking finds it difficult to change its position and the worker has no other solution than to institute legal proceedings.

Other machinery exists for the settlement of disputes: the joint committees or committees on interpretation which every collective labour agreement must provide for. These committees which, in accordance with the Workers' Charter, are authorised to consider the matters assigned to them may also be entrusted with the settlement of individual disputes. After having discussed their activities, the mission gathered the impression that they are effective as regards claims of a technical nature, in particular those concerning job classification. In other cases, however, they appear to be of lesser importance. This is probably due to the fact that their decisions are not final and do not prejudge those that may be taken by the judicial authorities, with which an appeal may always be lodged. The mission was told that the joint committees have played a much less important role than might have been expected.

COLLECTIVE DISPUTES

For many years collective disputes were not legally recognised in Spain. This did not, however, prevent the occurrence of such disputes and it was the responsibility of the government authorities and the trade union organisation itself to take appropriate measures to settle them.[2]

The fact of labour disputes was gradually recognised in successive legislation enacted under the previous regime, culminating in a decree of 1975 [3] which authorised strikes, although they were subject to a stringent procedure. A Spanish author has pointed out that the excessive number of obstacles imposed by the law explains why the numerous strike movements which occurred while Legislative Decree No. 5 of May 1975 was in force systematically ignored its provisions.[4]

In subsequent years, the number of labour disputes rose in 1978 and 1979, fell sharply in 1980 and has since remained at a level which the public authorities and the social partners consider very moderate, with a renewed rise occurring in 1983. Table 5 illustrates this trend.

Various reasons were advanced to explain the trend, some of which have already been referred to in the chapter on collective bargaining. The mission was informed on a number of occasions that the period of transition was marked by an increase in the number of politically inspired disputes, which later fell abruptly when after long years of dictatorship the normal means of political expression in a democratic State were finally recognised. In addition, wage negotiations based on the framework agreements, combined with the determination of the social partners to achieve mutual recognition and to assure more settled industrial relations, undoubtedly helped significantly to reduce the number of disputes. However, they increased in 1983, mainly on account of three factors (setting aside the public sector problems which are dealt with elsewhere): workforce reductions due to industrial redeployment; delays in payment of wages; and the application of the Act on the 40-hour working week. At the beginning of 1984, the CEOE stated that 78.37 million hours were lost in 1983, an increase of 35.51 per cent over 1982 (57.8 million hours), although the number of hours lost through disputes strictly related to labour issues was considerably lower: 38.76 million in 1983, compared with 29.85 million in 1982.[5]

Methods of settlement

Collective disputes on rights

Spanish authors use this term to describe disputes on the interpretation of an existing regulation and affecting an entire group of workers. Such disputes often give rise to direct action. Nevertheless, they may be settled through a "collective labour disputes" procedure, though if workers avail themselves of this procedure they may not exercise the right to strike.[6]

Suits involving collective disputes on rights must be instituted with the administrative authority (i.e. the General Labour Directorate, provincial departments of the Ministry of Labour or the competent authorities of the autonomous communities where competence has already been transferred to them). The labour authority must convene the parties to endeavour to bring about an amicable settlement or to propose voluntary arbitration. If no

Table 5. Labour disputes in Spain, 1976-83

Item	Year							
	1976	1977	1978	1979	1980	1981	1982	1983
No. of disputes	3 662	1 194	1 128	2 680	2 103	2 201	1 965	1 926
No. of workers concerned (thousands)	2 556.4	2 955	3 863	5 713.2	2 287	2 005.7	1 182	1 215.54
No. of working days lost (thousands))	12 593	16 642	11 551	18 917	6 177.5	5 154.5	2 786	3 876.25

Sources. For 1976-82, ILO: *Year Book of Labour Statistics 1983* (Geneva, 1983); for 1983, CEOC (disputes strictly related to labour issues).

settlement is reached, the party concerned may institute proceedings with the judicial authority and in this case, as in that of the procedure governing individual disputes, an attempt at conciliation, which may include mediation, must first be made through the IMAC. If attempts at conciliation fail, the party concerned may submit the dispute to the judicial labour authority, whose decision is final and binding.

Recent experience has shown that in Spain conciliation in collective disputes on points of law is successful in only a very small proportion of cases. According to the IMAC's figures, there were in 1981 163 cases of conciliation where a settlement was reached, 1,680 cases where no settlement was reached and 522 cases which failed because one of the parties did not attend the hearing; in 1982 the corresponding figures were 103, 1,418 and 639 and, for the first nine months of 1983, 128, 1,317 and 488. Fewer than 10 per cent of collective disputes on points of law, therefore, are settled through conciliation at the IMAC. The chief explanation for what may appear on the face of it to be an unsatisfactory performance is perhaps that the parties consider it necessary to submit their dispute to the labour courts, as a decision by the courts has the advantage of providing a legal guarantee in respect of similar cases which might arise in the future. This may also explain the meagre success of the joint committees established under collective labour agreements, since the courts themselves have made it clear that the committees' decisions are in no way a substitute for judicial authority and are without prejudice to a court decision.

As in the case of individual disputes, it is essentially the labour courts which are called upon to settle collective disputes on rights. On a visit to the Central Labour Court, the mission learned that the Court has a specialised division to deal with such disputes, of which it settles about 500-600 each year.

Apart from this official machinery, the labour inspectors also play an unofficial role in mediation and conciliation. These officials, held in high regard in Spain, are responsible mainly for enforcement of labour regulations: the opening or alteration of undertakings; employment injuries; job classification; incentives; working methods and so on. The labour inspector is in general very much respected by employers and workers on account of his competence and impartiality. The parties therefore frequently request him to act as a mediator both in disputes on points of law and in conflicts of interests; thanks to his personal competence and to his knowledge not only of the regulations but also of the actual working conditions in each undertaking, his proposals are often accepted and his mediation successful. Because of its unofficial character, this type of mediation is not covered by statistics relating to either disputes or settlements. Judging from the information received, however, labour inspectors help to settle a large number of collective disputes without direct action needing to be taken or formal proceedings instituted.

Conflicts of interests

In the system of labour relations in Spain, conflicts of interests, or "economic disputes", are those in which the protagonists are, on the one hand, a group of workers and, on the other, an employer or group of employers (whether or not represented by an occupational association) and which concern an issue not covered by laws or collective agreements, or that may be covered by provisions that it is a question of changing.

Unlike collective disputes on points of law, "economic" disputes cannot be settled by the labour courts, which are not competent in the matter. It is therefore appropriate to consider the rules and procedures governing the settlement of such disputes.

Compulsory arbitration

After a long period under the previous regime in which conflicts of interests were purely and simply ignored by the law, an interventionist settlements procedure was established under the 1958 Act on collective bargaining, which set up a machinery to issue "compulsory arbitration awards". The system then in operation was maintained by the 1973 Act respecting collective trade union agreements.

It was during the period of transition to democracy that the Royal Legislative Decree of 1977 on labour relations already referred to was enacted, which maintained compulsory arbitration awards for issues examined under the collective disputes procedure instituted at the request of one or other of the parties.[7] The legislative decree also provided for compulsory arbitration imposed by the public authorities "having regard to the duration and consequences of a strike, the attitudes of the parties and any serious prejudice to the national economy". All these provisions were applied quite frequently from 1977 to 1981, as shown in table 6.

The actual number of awards given has never been high compared with the number of collective agreements. However, the number of workers concerned is considerable; for example, in 1977 it represented 21.3 per cent of the total number of workers in units subject to collective bargaining provisions.[8] By way of comparison, in the last year of the Franco regime (1975), 189 compulsory arbitration awards concerning 915,419 workers were issued (in the same year 1,027 collective agreements were concluded covering 1,818,788 workers).[9] It will

Table 6. Compulsory arbitration awards, 1977-81

Item	Year				
	1977	1978	1979	1980	1981 [1]
No. of awards	206	82	125	125	56
No. of workers concerned	613 512	374 258	904 599	517 824	623 124

[1] Data available up to March.
Source. General Directorate of Labour.

be seen from these figures that in Spain the settlement of conflicts of interests was for many years subject to considerable outside pressure, which began to diminish with the change of regime but which had by no means disappeared in 1981.

The Constitutional Court's ruling of 8 April 1981 brought about a complete change. It was the Court's view that compulsory arbitration awards issued in connection with a collective disputes procedure instituted by one of the parties encroached upon the right to collective bargaining established under article 37 of the Constitution. However, it considered that compulsory arbitration by the public authorities to end a strike that might cause prejudice to the national economy did not constitute a violation of the right to strike recognised under article 28 of the Constitution, provided that the requirement was met that the arbitrators be impartial.

The practical effect of this ruling was that compulsory arbitration virtually disappeared. As regards disputes which might cause serious prejudice to the national economy — the only case in which there may be compulsory arbitration today — only one or two awards have been issued since 1981. In one of the cases, which concerned service stations covered by the petrol monopoly, the Director General of Labour, who was designated as an arbitrator, first made a fresh attempt to arrange negotiations before issuing a compulsory arbitration award on 28 August 1981. The mission was told by the public authorities that it was their firm intention to avoid compulsory arbitration whenever possible, employing it only in extremely serious cases.

Voluntary mediation and arbitration

Mediation may be initiated on the basis of a provision of the Workers' Charter which lays down that at any time during collective bargaining the parties may have recourse to a mediator designated by them. In addition, the decree establishing the IMAC provides that the parties may request the Institute to appoint such a mediator.

However, mediation, or at least what might be referred to as "formal" mediation, has not yet become fully established in Spain. The IMAC's statistics show that the number of cases of mediation remains below that of cases of conciliation in collective rights disputes: 66 in 1981, only half of which were successful; 64 in 1982 (38 successful) and 36 in the first nine months of 1983 (25 successful). There is insufficient data concerning cases of private mediation, but the mission was informed that private mediation is not a customary procedure and here too the number of cases would appear to be limited.

Nevertheless, a very large number of unofficial cases of mediation occur, which do not appear in the statistics. As was pointed out in the chapter on collective bargaining, the chairmen of bargaining committees, when such committees are established, often act as de facto mediators in making proposals to the parties. In the case of more commonplace disputes not necessarily connected with the negotiation of a collective agreement, the labour inspector also acts as a mediator and the social partners stated that they considered his role to be a very positive one. Despite the fact that inspection involves supervision and law enforcement, which in other countries are considered to be incompatible with conciliation activity,[10] it appears that in Spain the two functions may be combined without giving rise to serious difficulties. In short, though formal mediation by a specialised public official has not yet gained the kind of favour in Spain that it enjoys in other countries, there are other forms of mediation which so far appear to play an effective role. It is possible in any case that in future a full-time mediation service will be introduced, either in a decentralised form through the industrial relations boards or in the form of state legislation to regulate the settlement of labour disputes.

Voluntary arbitration — the only authorised form of arbitration apart from arbitration of disputes which may cause serious prejudice — is not much practised in Spain, although it is not unknown: in 1982, 14 cases of arbitration concerning 66,895 workers were recorded; in 1983, there were nine cases involving 27,552 undertakings and 69,752 workers.[11] The number of cases of arbitration, then, is extremely low compared with the number of collective agreements and disputes. There are no doubt social, political and even psychological reasons for this. In the first place, official arbitration became discredited in Spain as it was employed prematurely and to excess during the period of state interventionism. For the same reason, voluntary arbitration has never managed to become established. As the former has practically disappeared, the latter would remain the only valid solution. However, as voluntary arbitration lacks what some described as the "seal of authority", it would appear difficult to enforce compliance by the parties. It is perhaps for this reason that the second congress of the CCOO came out in favour of the IMAC's role as an arbitrator when the parties failed to reach agreement in the course of collective bargaining.[12]

Thus, there is at present a deficiency in the final phase of the disputes settlement procedure. This shortcoming has been made good in a few cases by the extension of collective agreements, a matter dealt with in the previous chapter. However, the extension of agreements is a limited and controversial method which the employers have strongly criticised and certain unions regard as inadequate. Despite this, the absence of an arbitration procedure acceptable to the social partners has not yet given rise to any major difficulty because it has coincided with a period of social collaboration and reduced intensity of disputes. This deficiency might well be felt much more strongly if the frequency of open disputes, which was low at the time of the mission, were to increase.

Settlement procedures established by the parties themselves

The establishment of procedures by the parties themselves might constitute a means of overcoming the above-mentioned institutional deficiency. In 1983, the CEOE appeared to agree with the UGT and the CCOO on this approach to the problem; the Inter-Confederation Agreement concluded that year accordingly states that the signatory organisations agree that voluntary mediation and arbitration procedures should be encouraged in order to settle collective labour disputes. For this purpose, it goes on to say, the Inter-Confederation Joint Committee will, by unanimous decision, establish rules for voluntary mediation and arbitration and will draw up a list of arbitrators and mediators to be made available to the parties to disputes. At the same time, certain industrial relations boards were engaged in the preparation of standard clauses of similar content for inclusion in collective labour agreements negotiated in the autonomous communities concerned. However, at the end of 1983 none of these initiatives had produced tangible results.

Direct action

We have already referred to the observations made by the competent bodies of the ILO regarding the prohibition of strikes under the previous regime. In 1977 a legislative decree [13] recognised the right of the workers to have recourse to this means of action and the right of employers to resort to lock-outs, although it imposed a series of restrictions. After the adoption in 1978 of the Constitution, which expressly guaranteed the right to strike [14] — and, though somewhat less explicitly, to lock out — the Constitutional Court was called upon to examine the legality of the strike provisions of the legislative decree. This it did in its ruling of 8 April 1981, already mentioned, which confirmed the legal validity of a number of the sections of the legislative decree, declared others null and void and amended still others.[15]

The new legislation at present in preparation is expected to deal with the question comprehensively. Nevertheless, at least where strikes are concerned, the unions seem rather to favour what they refer to as "self-regulation", namely restrictions on this right which the persons concerned impose on themselves.[16] The Minister of Labour and Social Security, Mr. Joaquín Almunia, made it quite clear to the mission that the new provisions would be adopted only in agreement with the social partners, since in an area of this nature such agreement was particularly necessary for the proper application of the legal texts.

Here again the present period appears to be one of transition in which uncertainties and legal controversies abound. Without going into these in detail, it is nevertheless indispensable to indicate a few salient points and to give a brief analysis of the legal possibilities for direct action open to workers or employers, before examining how disputes operate in practice.

Regulations governing strikes

As we have seen, the Constitution recognises the right of workers to strike in defence of their interests. This right may be suspended only during a state of siege or emergency.[17] The Constitution adds that specific guarantees must be established to ensure the maintenance of essential services to the community. The legislative decree of 1977 contains provisions in this sense [18] which should be interpreted in the light of the Constitutional Court ruling.

According to the ruling, the Government may, taking into account the duration or the consequences of a strike, of the attitude of the parties and of the seriousness of the damage to the national economy, order the dispute to be referred to an impartial arbitration body. Moreover, strikes by workers in strategic sectors for the purpose of disrupting production are deemed to be unlawful or unwarranted until proof has been obtained to the contrary. The Government has also the power to impose the necessary measures to ensure the smooth operation of services essential to the community, subject to the jurisdiction of the courts of justice.

Both the Committee on Freedom of Association and the ILO Committee of Experts on the Application of Conventions and Recommendations have commented on these provisions. In particular, they have recalled that denial or restriction of the right to strike should be permissible only in the case of public services or essential services in the strict sense, namely those whose interruption could endanger the existence or well-being of the whole or part of the population.[19]

Workers in essential services are not alone in not enjoying the right to strike. This is of course the case with those who are unable to organise. Restrictions can also be noted for other categories of persons. Thus, under the Penal Code, those responsible for providing any kind of public or recognised essential service who disorganise it or impair its regularity in any way by suspending their activity are deemed guilty of sedition.[20] This provision expressly refers to a wider range of services than the essential services to which we have just referred. The question arises whether it refers to the civil service as a whole. Many consider that it does but, as we shall see in the next chapter, many strikes nevertheless take place in this sector and apparently remain unpunished.

Special legislation also limits the possibilities of direct action in the merchant navy and in civil aviation [21] and lays down specific conditions for the exercise of such action in sectors such as public hospitals [22] or the national railways.[23]

In the last two sectors, and also, for example, in respect of the airline company Iberia, the port services, electricity undertakings and the post and telecommunications services, the authorities may organise a minimum service which must operate during work stoppages, and determine the means by which this is to be done. The application of such measures has encountered keen opposition from all the trade union confederations that the mission met. This was undeniably one of the points on which their relations with the Government were the most strained at the time of its visit.

Complaints have also been lodged with the ILO Committee on Freedom of Association in connection with disputes in the hospital services and RENFE. In the former case, the Committee stressed in particular the importance of ensuring that the provisions respecting the minimum service to be ensured in the event of a strike in an essential service should be clearly stated, strictly applied and known to all concerned well in advance.[24]

In the case of RENFE, the legislation empowers the authorities to require railwaymen to obey requisition orders when this is considered necessary. Furthermore, under the circulars for its application, the authorities may make extensive use of the powers which they have been granted. The Committee on Freedom of Association pointed to the possibilities of abuse inherent in the requisitioning of workers as a means of settling labour disputes; it went on to say that recourse to measures of this kind was undesirable, except for the purpose of maintaining essential services in circumstances of acute national emergency. The Committee was nevertheless aware that a total and prolonged stoppage of railway services throughout the country might lead to a situation such as to endanger the well-being of the population and saw some justification in maintaining a minimum service if the extent and duration of a strike were such as to provoke an acute national emergency. In order to be acceptable, it stated, a minimum service of this kind should be restricted to operations strictly necessary to avoid endangering the existence or well-being of the whole or part of the population on the one hand and, on the other, workers' organisations should be able to participate in defining such a service in the same way as employers and the public authorities.[25]

It is clear that problems have not yet been overcome in this sector: during a strike which occurred shortly before the mission's visit, the authorities set a level of 80 per cent for the minimum service to be assured by personnel whose work was connected with the actual running of the trains. All the trade union federations protested vigorously against these measures. Speaking in more general terms of the obligation to maintain a minimum service in certain branches of activity, certain trade union officials, particularly in the UGT, regretted that there had been no genuine consultations with the unions on the definition of a minimum service.

The Legislative Decree of 1977, which has often been quoted, also contains various provisions on the procedure to be followed in the event of a strike. Certain of these have either been declared null and void or interpreted restrictively by the Constitutional Court ruling of 8 April 1981. It would be superfluous to examine them in detail for present purposes. Suffice it to say that the advance notice to be given is, in principle, five days [26] during which the strike committee must guarantee the services necessary to ensure the safety of persons and property and the maintenance of premises, machinery, installations and raw materials, and take any other measures necessary to enable the undertaking to resume its activities.[27]

The Legislative Decree also deems unlawful [28] any strike whose purpose is to change the provisions of a collective agreement or an award currently in force. The Constitutional Court considered this provision to be constitutional in so far as it is interpreted in such a way as to permit the holding of strikes whose purpose is not to change a collective agreement in the strict sense but, for example, to demand an interpretation or to present claims not involving a revision of the agreement; it should even be possible for a strike to attempt to change an agreement if the employer or the employers' association has failed to honour its commitments or if radical changes have occurred in the situation since the time when the agreement was signed. Although authors working in this area in Spain regard the "peace obligation" (i.e. an undertaking not to stop work as a means of action) as implicit in all collective agreements,[29] as the mission was told by many of its exponents, this obligation appears very limited unless, of course, the parties themselves deliberately decide to extend it.[30]

Staggered strikes, "go-slows" and, more generally, any collective disturbance of work "otherwise than in the form of a strike" in the traditional sense, are deemed to be unwarranted.[31] According to those the mission spoke to, these forms of strikes are infrequent, except perhaps for working to rule in the civil service. They cited an instance of working to rule by policemen which appeared unlawful on two accounts — as an instance of working to rule and as a policemen's strike — but no penalty was imposed on the persons concerned.

Strikers may publicise their action in a peaceful manner and may collect funds for the purpose, but without resorting to any coercion, and they must respect the freedom of employment of any workers who do not wish to be associated with a strike; [32] otherwise they may be prosecuted in the Penal Courts.[33] Strike pickets may accordingly — and this is a practice which seems to be spreading, particularly in the construction industry — peaceably incite other workers to keep away from their workplace, but picketing may not be accompanied by coercion or other forms of violence in an attempt to interfere with freedom of work.[34] It should also be added that the parties to the Inter-Confederation Framework Agreement of 1980 undertook to promote a policy of non-violence against persons and property. The mission was also told that strikers tend to occupy the workplace more often in agricultural undertakings than in factories or offices. This form of action is generally regarded as unlawful.[35] The mission nevertheless learned of an instance of occupation of a post office in which no penalty appeared to have been imposed on the persons concerned.

As has been seen, the Constitution recognises the right of workers to strike in defence of their interests. The Legislative Decree of 1977 stipulates that a strike is unlawful if it is begun or continued for political reasons or for any other purpose unconnected with the occupational interests of the workers concerned. The same applies to a sympathy strike which is not even indirectly related to the occupational interests of the persons beginning or continuing it.[36] Finally, under the Penal Code employers and workers who undermine the authority of the State or disorganise its normal activity by suspending work or disrupting its regular progress with the intention of undermining the security of the State are deemed to be guilty of sedition.[37] The mission did not hear of any case in which this provision had been applied.

In Spain the right to strike is regarded as an individual right which, if lawfully exercised, involves nothing more than a suspension of the contract of employment; [38] it does not give rise to any penalty nor does it have the effect of terminating employment, unless the worker has taken an active part in an illegal work stoppage.[39] Nevertheless, the mission was told that an employer may seek by various means to dismiss a striker, particularly if he considers him to be a "leader"; for example, he may allow a certain time to pass and dismiss him when the links between the dismissal and the dispute have become more difficult to establish. The problem is part of that of protection against acts of anti-union discrimination discussed in an earlier chapter. Anyone who prevents or restricts the lawful exercise of freedom of association or the right to strike is liable to a penalty under the Penal Code.[40] Many of those with whom the mission spoke, however, stressed that strikes — even illegal strikes, in the view of some — had now become part of the Spanish way of life and that reprisals seemed to be relatively infrequent.

While a strike is in progress, the employer may not replace the strikers by workers who were not connected with the undertaking when notice of the strike was given.[41] However, CCOO officials told the mission that such practices were occasionally resorted to.

Conditions for the exercise of the right to lock out

The Constitution also recognises the employer's right to organise a lock-out.[42] Unlike the right to strike, this right is not regarded as a basic right and does not enjoy such extensive guarantees; admittedly, the question of protection is not posed in the same terms.

The Legislative Decree of 1977 devotes a number of sections to work stoppages at the initiative of the employer.[43] The only lock-outs authorised, the mission was told, are defensive ones, namely those organised in response to a strike or other form of collective disruption of work. Furthermore, the law requires certain special circumstances to be met before an employer can resort to this means of action: there must be a manifest danger of violence to persons or serious damage to property; the workplace or any related premises must have been unlawfully occupied (or there must be a definite risk that they will be so occupied); or the scale of absenteeism or irregularities in the performance of the work must seriously prejudice the normal course of production. These conditions set strict limits on the possibilities of recourse to lock-outs. Moreover, a lock-out may not last for longer than the period necessary to ensure the resumption of work in the undertaking or remove the causes that gave rise to it. The employer must reopen the workplace and offer his workers an opportunity of resuming their employment if he is ordered to do so by the labour authority.

The practice of strikes or lock-outs

Immediately after the right to strike was recognised, many severe work stoppages occurred. Nevertheless, all the persons whom the mission met — whether in employers', trade union, government or university circles — agreed that there was a marked defusing of social tension with the conclusion of the Inter-Confederation Framework Agreement in the early days of 1980 and of the subsequent national inter-occupational agreements. This, the mission was told at CEOE headquarters, permitted the consolidation of a socially stable Spanish democracy. The figures cited in table 5 confirm this trend. The fact that, as remarked above, procedures for the peaceful settlement of disputes (conciliation, mediation and arbitration) do not function very effectively may explain the persistence of some of these disputes. The causes of other disputes lie, according to employers' circles, in conflicts between trade unions and in the tendency of some of them to shift to the level of the undertaking an opposition which is essentially of a political nature. Lock-outs do occur but they are rare, according to observers.

Certain trade union officials encountered, however, referred to latent conflicts or even a revival of social tension linked with employment problems and industrial redeployment. The statistics published by the Ministry of Labour and Social Security show, moreover, a slight increase in the incidence of strikes for the first six months of 1983 compared with the same period in 1982: 1,564 strikes against 1,489, 1,251,700 workers affected against 1,037,700.[44] The statistics published by the CEOE for 1983 confirm this trend.[45] There was also an increase in the number of disputes during the first months of 1984 after the failure of efforts to conclude a framework agreement for the year. It should be added that strikes of a certain magnitude are often accompanied by demonstrations and that sympathy strikes are frequent.

Notes

[1] Codified text of the Act respecting the procedure to be followed in labour suits, *Boletín Oficial del Estado*, 30 July 1980.

[2] ILO: *The labour and trade union situation in Spain* (Geneva, 1969), p. 211.

[3] Legislative Decree No. 5 of 22 May 1975 respecting the settlement of collective labour disputes.

[4] Alfredo Montoya Melgar: *Derecho del trabajo* (Madrid, Editoral Tecnos, 1981), p. 598.

[5] CEOE: *Datos estadísticos significativos en materia laboral correspondientes a 1983* (Madrid, Jan. 1984), p. 16.

[6] See Royal Legislative Decree No. 17 of 4 March 1977 respecting labour relations, section 17. This text provides that, where a strike has been called, the workers may cancel it and avail themselves of the collective disputes procedure. This procedure may also be instituted at the employer's request but in this case, if the workers exercise their right to strike, the procedure is suspended and the file closed.

[7] In practice, these provisions could only apply to collective disputes procedures instituted by the workers since, if a procedure was instituted at the employer's request and the workers called a strike, it was suspended and the file closed.

[8] General Directorate of Economic Policy and Forecasting, Ministry of Economy and Commerce: *Un análisis estructural de los convenios colectivos: 1980-81* (Madrid, 1982), pp. 48-52.

[9] Source: Central Office of Collective Agreements.

[10] See also article 3, para. 2, of the Labour Inspection Convention, 1947 (No. 81).

[11] Data supplied by the General Directorate of Labour.

[12] See *Gaceta Sindical*, Cuadernos G.S., No. 3, p. 41.

[13] Royal Legislative Decree No. 17 of 4 March 1977 respecting labour relations.

[14] The Workers' Charter Act subsequently included the right to strike among the basic rights of workers (section 4, 1 *(e)*).

[15] See in particular *Official Bulletin*, 1981, Series B, No. 2, 208th Report of the Committee on Freedom of Association, Case No. 874, paras. 78 ff.

[16] The CCOO, for example, have issued directives on the conditions for strikes in the public service: see II Congreso de la Confederación sindical de CCOO: "La acción sindical de CCOO ante la crisis y el paro", in *Gaceta Sindical*, Cuaderno G.S. No. 3, pp. 36-37.

[17] Articles 28 and 55, para. 1, of the Constitution.

[18] In particular, section 7 (2) and section 10.

[19] See *Official Bulletin*, 1981, Series B, No. 2, 208th Report of the Committee on Freedom of Association, Case No. 874, paras. 82 ff.

[20] Section 222 of the Penal Code, as amended.

[21] Act of 22 December 1955 (merchant navy) and Penal and Procedural Act of 1964 respecting civil aviation; see, in this connection, A. Ojeda Avilés: *Derecho sindical* (Madrid, Editorial Tecnos, 1980), pp. 317-318.

[22] Royal Decree No. 156 of 2 February 1979.

[23] Royal Decree No. 266 of 8 February 1980.

[24] See 233rd Report of the Committee on Freedom of Association, Case No. 1203, paras. 89 to 96, 225th Session of the Governing Body of the ILO (doc. GB.225/9/9).

[25] See *Official Bulletin*, 1980, Series B, No. 3, 204th Report of the Committee on Freedom of Association, Case No. 952, paras. 157 to 164. In a ruling of 17 July 1981, the Constitutional Court declared null and void one of the circulars for the application of Royal Decree No. 266 guaranteeing the operation of the public railway service entrusted to RENFE.

[26] Section 3 (3). The Constitutional Court considered that it was not necessary to observe this period of notice in the event of *force majeure* or an emergency.

[27] Section 6 (7), as interpreted by the Constitutional Court.

[28] Section 11 *(c)*; see also article 37, para. 1, of the Constitution and section 82 of the 1980 Workers' Charter Act.

[29] See also M. Alonso Olea: *El estatuto de los trabajadores: Texto y comentario breve* (Madrid, Civitas, 1980), p. 256, and Ojeda Avilés, op. cit, p. 412.

[30] See section 80 (2) of the 1980 Workers' Charter Act.

[31] Section 7 (2) of Royal Legislative Decree No. 17 of 4 March 1977, as interpreted by the Constitutional Court.

[32] ibid., section 6, subsections (4) and (6).

[33] Section 496 of the Penal Code, as amended.

[34] See, in this connection, *Official Bulletin*, 1979, Series B, No. 3, 197th Report of the Committee on Freedom of Association, Cases Nos. 923 and 915, paras. 58 and 473.

[35] But see I. Garcia-Perrote Escartín: *La huelga con ocupación de lugar del trabajo* (Madrid, Akal, 1981).

[36] Section 11 *(a)* and *(b)*, as interpreted by the Constitutional Court.

[37] Section 222 (2), as amended.

[38] Section 6 (2) of the Legislative Decree of 1977.

[39] See sections 6 (1), and 33 *(j)* and *(k)*, of the Legislative Decree of 1977.

[40] Section 177*bis* of the Penal Code.

[41] Section 6 (5) of the Legislative Decree of 1977.

[42] Article 37 (2).

[43] Sections 12 to 15 of the Legislative Decree of 1977.

[44] *Boletín de estadísticas laborales*, Aug.-Sep. 1983, p. 57.

[45] CEOE: *Conflictividad laboral* (Madrid, Dec. 1983), p. 4.

INDUSTRIAL RELATIONS IN THE PUBLIC SECTOR 8

THE PUBLIC SERVICE

Although trade unionism first made an appearance in the public service at the beginning of the century, one can speak of the existence of genuine industrial relations only as of about 1980, since before that date, and especially during the Franco era, the links between the administration and its employees were arranged in far too statutory and hierarchical a manner for such relations to be possible. Moreover, certain provisions in force during this period, for example the Trade Union Act of February 1971, debarred from trade union membership all public servants, that is to say all persons bound to the public administration by the provision of remunerated services governed by administrative laws. In fact, the prohibition on the establishment of unions in the public service dated back to a decree of January 1936.

As of 1976, the establishment of industrial relations in the public service started spontaneously in practice, but somewhat cautiously as far as legislation was concerned. First by force of circumstances, and later by political choice, the institutional framework gradually changed as the need was felt to accept in the public service certain industrial relations procedures which had developed in the private sector.

Summary regulations governing the rights of association of civil servants were introduced in mid-1976 and an Act was adopted at the end of the same year on the participation and collaboration of public servants in the bodies responsible for the regulation and administration of the public service. It was thus recognised that labour problems in the public service could no longer be settled in accordance with the old administrative procedures.

Royal Decree No. 1522 of 17 June 1977, referred to in Chapter 3, made provision for the exercise by public servants of the right to associate in trade unions. The decree also provided that organisations of public servants might, through consultation and collaboration procedures, participate in determining their conditions of employment.

However, this Royal Decree did not cover the right to collective bargaining; its major significance arises perhaps out of its acceptance of the principle of representation and of the defence of public servants' organisations, and its recognition of the distinct nature of trade unionism in the case of public servants, as compared with the general regulations governing the right of association issued in April of the same year.

In 1978, the Constitution recognised the right of public servants freely to join a trade union, but made provision for the legislature to regulate the "special features" of the exercise of this right. This recognition, expressed in two articles of the Constitution (articles 28 and 103.3) gave fresh impetus to trade unionism in the public service, and the following years witnessed a veritable proliferation of union organisations. Some merely replaced the former associations, while others were of a completely new type; most were associated with the major trade union confederations but a number of them declared themselves independent, and this gave rise to a certain amount of concern in the confederations.[1] Trade unionism expanded in particular in education and the postal and health services. As regards the police, although discussions were still continuing as to whether unarmed superintendents and inspectors should be able or not to form unions and whether this right should be extended to the municipal police forces, a large number of union organisations of national scope had already been established.[2] However, membership rates varied enormously, as certain branches of the public service were still rather unfavourably disposed to trade union activity and maintained a "corporatist mentality far removed from trade unionism and, in particular, class trade unionism".[3] The expansion of trade unionism was facilitated by a circular of 1977 in which the Government accepted trade union activities throughout the public administration, at both the national and local level and in the autonomous institutions, and provided facilities for such activities. Further provisions were introduced subsequently to regulate the right of public servants to collective representation and their right of assembly.[4]

It was, however, more difficult to introduce bargaining and to gain acceptance of direct action measures in the public service. The Constitution, which was explicit in respect of freedom of association, referred to collective bargaining and strikes only in general terms and without any explicit mention of public servants. For its part, the Workers' Charter excluded from its scope both the employment of public servants, which was to be governed by future Public Service Rules, and that of persons working in the service of the State, local authorities and independent public bodies if, by virtue of any law, such employment was governed by administrative provisions or rules.

Public servants' organisations developed for several years in the shadow of a constitutional principle that was not backed by regulations and of legislation which failed to define the limits of trade union action. The new trends appeared to recognise the divergence of interests within the administration, but the legislation in force remained silent as regards the possibility to be offered to public servants for the conclusion of genuine collective agreements.

In addition, no provision was made for procedures governing the exercise by public servants of the right to strike, in spite of the fact that Spain, by ratifying the European Social Charter which implicitly recognises this right, appeared to be in favour of it.[5] However, some experts pointed out to the mission that Spain ratified the Charter with certain reservations, particularly with regard to article 6 which deals, among other matters, with the right to strike. The question gave rise to a debate on the reason that might justify the granting or refusal of the right to bargain and the right to strike in the case of public servants. According to some authors, the absence of a specific reference in the Constitution does not preclude the extension to the public service of all the rights of collective autonomy laid down in the Constitution; [6] in the opinion of others, the term "worker" used in articles 28 and 37 of the Constitution should be understood in the broad sense, without any distinction between public law, which regulates the employment of public servants, and private law governing contracts of employment. With regard to collective bargaining, there appeared to be a feeling that the resulting agreements should be regarded as "typical arrangements" without any precise legal equivalent.[7] As to strikes, the idea was emerging that the right to strike applied to all workers in the private and public sectors, with certain inevitable restrictions in the case of the armed forces.

In the opinion of the Committee of Experts on the Application of Conventions and Recommendations, restrictions on the right to strike should only apply to the public service in the strict sense of the term (or the essential services already referred to) and the exercise of the right to strike should be confined to public servants acting in that capacity as agents of the public authority.[8]

At all events, the theoretical debate lagged behind actual practice. Collective bargaining was becoming generalised, even though its importance varied according to whether the categories of persons employed in the public service were working in auxiliary services, under contract, or had the status of public servants. In the first case, collective bargaining was frequent and led to the conclusion of genuine collective agreements; this occurred in several ministries and on two occasions (July 1982 and March 1984) collective bargaining even led to the conclusion of framework agreements on the working conditions and bargaining rights of persons employed in the auxiliary services of the public service. However, there was no genuine collective bargaining in the case of persons under contract, despite their union activity in defence of their interests. Similarly, as regards public servants, in the absence of bargaining procedures agreements were concluded on a more or less unofficial basis in certain independent state bodies, such as the social security administration, and in certain local government administrations, and unofficial negotiations were held on certain salary increments and on the organisation of working hours in the ministries. A national agreement was concluded in March 1982 between the public administration and three trade union federations representing public servants — the CCOO, the Independent Trade Union Confederation of Public Servants (CSIF) and the Federation of Public Administration Workers (FETAP).[9] The agreement related to programmes to improve the efficiency and productivity of the public service and to raise certain increments and salaries.[10] In 1983, the same parties signed an agreement of broader scope, more in the nature of a collective bargaining agreement, which provided for salary increases, rationalisation of systems of remuneration and higher pensions. This agreement applied to all persons employed in the public service and its autonomous institutions, including public servants, and made provision for the opening of negotiations concerning teachers. According to the Federation of Public Services,[9] it was the "first agreement of general scope negotiated in the Spanish public service".[11]

The principle of the strike was also gaining ground in the public service. During the three weeks of the mission's visit, there were four strikes in the Spanish public service, involving the police, meteorological services, prison administration and certain local authorities. Generally speaking, there appeared to be two main reasons for strikes in the public service: the relative deterioration of working conditions in a category that had previously enjoyed a favourable position, and uncertainty with regard to the possibilities and objectives of bargaining. The impression was that industrial relations had made a breakthrough in the public service but that they continued to meet with difficulties owing to a lack of precise indications as to the course to be pursued.

The increasing difficulty encountered with regard to the problem of industrial relations in the public service had led to the establishment in 1978 of a State Secretariat for the Public Service at the Ministry of the Presidency of the Council. This initiative stemmed from the desire to centralise staff policy in the public service. Although the setting and co-ordination of objectives in the State Secretariat were theoretically entrusted to the General Directorate of the Public Service, it was in fact the Secretary of State, and often even the Minister of the Presidency, who personally supervised the consultations held with the public servants' unions on the staff policies of the central administration. Moreover, the practical management of industrial relations depended to a large extent on the initiative and style of each public service department, some of which enjoyed a certain amount of autonomy in the matter. Thus the General Directorate of Posts, which employed more than 60,000 persons, pursued a progressive policy which provided for guarantees in respect of welfare activities, time off for union functions, the setting up of representative committees at all levels and their active participation in determining conditions of employment.

As regards postal staff employed in auxiliary services, who do not have the status of public servants, participation took the form of collective bargaining: a national, regional or provincial collective agreement was concluded for each branch, the most important concerning employees in rural areas and in security, building maintenance and construction services.

In the case of public servants employed in the postal administration, participation was assured by committees composed of an equal number of members designated by the management and of public servants' representatives. Their main purpose was to participate in the drafting and revision of regulations governing the service and conditions of employment. With respect to the latter, the central and provincial committees take an active part in drawing up occupational safety and health and social assistance programmes, and supervise their implementation. They also act as advisory bodies to the General Directorate, to which they communicate the initiatives, suggestions and grievances of employees.

The mission was able to attend a meeting of a sub-committee at the central office dealing with the revision of such regulations and saw for itself the free and constructive atmosphere in which the work was carried out. Activities such as these take place without prejudice to the powers of the union organisations representing the administrative unit concerned. At the time, a strict system of recruitment by competition and advancement on merit was in operation, with salary increases in accordance with seniority, responsibility and occupational hazards or the arduous nature of the work carried out; there were also productivity incentive schemes and various indirect forms of remuneration. In the postal adminstration, as throughout the public service, earnings were adjusted each year in keeping with inflation and the general economic situation of the country by the General Budget Act. In spite of all these factors conducive to good industrial relations, a fairly widespread strike occurred in the postal administration in 1983.

Other public service departments were, however, less well disposed to this policy of dialogue with employees and continued to adopt the hierarchical approach which marked relations for so long in the past. Thus, in a substantial number of local authorities and certain ministries, union elections were not even held. The second congress of the CCOO in 1983 still included public servants among those who "had not yet acquired the right to negotiate".[12]

It was probably to avoid pursuing different objectives and to ensure uniform treatment in industrial relations in the public service that the Government extended the right to join trade unions, as provided for in the Bill on freedom of association approved in 1983, to workers engaged in public administration activities or with public service status. The new text was intended to unify the earlier provisions so as to permit the "gradual and progressive" development of the right to organise "through uniform regulations in a single text governing the exercise by public servants of the right to join trade unions".[13] This codification of the law could have a considerable impact on the exercise of the right to bargain collectively which, as has been seen, was still rather ill defined. The fact that the new Bill states clearly that trade union organisations, without any distinction, will enjoy the right to bargain collectively, to strike and to submit individual and collective complaints suggests that public servants will also be accorded the right to bargain, However, the same Bill, referring to the most representative organisations, indicates that public servants may "take part in discussions concerning the determination of conditions of employment in the public service in accordance with appropriate consultation or negotiation procedures". This possibility of a probably discretionary choice between two procedures gives the impression that bargaining may occur in certain cases but not in those for which the consultation procedure is selected.

The Labour Relations (Public Service) Convention, 1978 (No. 151), refers in

Article 7 to collective bargaining or "such other methods as will allow representatives of public employees to participate in the determination of these matters" (i.e terms and conditions of employment). It is therefore possible that the Government wishes to reserve the right to determine subsequently which categories or types of employees may bargain collectively as in the private sector, and which may be consulted through their unions or associations of public servants. It should be recalled that in the National Employment Agreement the Government recognised the principle of consultation and negotiation in the public service.[14] However, the question has not yet been finally resolved and could only be settled by specific legislation relating to public employees which defines clearly the type of participation, negotiation or consultation to be practised in the future.

PUBLIC UNDERTAKINGS

As far as industrial relations procedures are concerned, public undertakings are more akin to private undertakings than to the public service. The system of relations is in many respects the same as in the private sector and variations that exist are due not to differences in the recognised collective rights of workers but to the particular nature of a public undertaking. In principle, the general legal system of individual and collective labour relations is applied, and public undertakings are not excluded from the scope of the Workers' Charter; work contracts or employment relationships are established in accordance with the same provisions as for all other workers. Even if the regulations governing public undertakings envisaged at the end of 1983 are adopted, they are not expected to introduce restrictions or provisions that are appreciably different from legislation on private undertakings.

There are, however, a number of features — some common to all public undertakings, others peculiar to certain categories — which account for certain differences in industrial relations practice.

To begin with, public undertakings appeared to the mission to be more directly affected than others by state directives regarding wage increases and by other measures intended to strengthen the national economy. For historical or structural reasons, the majority of public undertakings experienced management, productivity or budget difficulties in 1983. Moreover, many of them, being engaged in activities that are not very profitable, had required large subsidies and were encountering serious redeployment problems.

The actual size of public undertakings has a bearing on industrial relations as it accentuates the seriousness of problems and strengthens the position of the trade unions. There are practically no small public undertakings, and the few medium-sized ones that exist are in general larger than the average undertaking in the private sector.[15] Public undertakings also differ from private ones in terms of sectoral distribution, since they operate for the most part in industry, mines, transport and other branches of activity which have always offered fertile ground for trade unionism.

It can therefore be readily understood why public undertakings have played such an important role in the development of industrial relations. During the boom that preceded the energy crisis, public undertakings played a pioneering role in gaining recognition of certain collective rights and the promotion of employment. There do not at present appear to be any serious obstacles to the development of trade unionism in state undertakings. Certain large public undertakings, such as the national railways (RENFE), have a long trade union tradition and the rate of union membership is over 50 per cent. The two major trade union confederations, the CCOO and the UGT, are more firmly established in the public than in the private sector, as is shown by the fact that two-thirds of the representatives engaged in negotiations in 1982 were affiliated to one or the other. However, although a considerable number of public undertakings (48 per cent) are members of the CEOE employers' organisation, the percentage is well below the figure given for private undertakings.

A study carried out in 1983 by the Ministry of Economy and Finance has shown that there are also differences in the public sector as regards collective bargaining. Negotiations are less protracted than in the private sector and often less contentious, judging from the number of hours per worker lost each year on account of strikes (3.64 in the public sector as compared to 5.29 in the private sector).[16] Although this may be explained by the greater security of employment and higher average wages in public undertakings, the situation began to change in 1982 and 1983. The percentage of employees not covered by collective agreement, which until recently was higher in the public than in the private sector, has tended over the last two years to move towards the figure for the private sector. These findings demonstrate an increasing uniformity of treatment of workers in both sectors.

The CCOO has sometimes criticised the management of public undertakings for adopting a tough position when negotiating collective agreements, for bargaining on occasion below the levels established in basic agreements or for failing to make concrete offers.[17] At the beginning of 1984, however, the cause of tension was above all the fact that no basic agreement had been reached for 1984 to provide guidance for negotiations and, as far as wages are concerned, the difficulty of reconciling the aspirations of workers, who wish to protect their purchasing power, with the current unfavourable economic situation.

The particular characteristics of certain undertakings also have an impact on industrial relations in such areas as decision-making, the limitations imposed by instructions, salary scales and regulations, and the minimum level of essential services. How strongly these issues are affected depends on the nature of the undertaking concerned.

Two types of undertaking may be distinguished in this respect: on the one hand, those operating in the agricultural, mining, industrial, commercial or services sectors, which all come more or less directly under the authority of the INI, an autonomous state administration founded in 1941; on the other hand, those providing a public service under the jurisdiction of a ministry, such as transport, communications, and gas and electricity. The second group includes some of the largest Spanish undertakings, such as RENFE which has more than 70,000 employees. The INI now covers some 200 undertakings employing a total of 220,000 persons (or 7 per cent of the active population) and accounting for about 17 per cent of the gross domestic product. The INI is thus the largest holding group in Spain; there are other state holding groups, such as the National Petroleum Institute. Of lesser importance are the undertakings attached to the Estates Service, some of which it took over to prevent their going bankrupt.

INI undertakings are independent as regards industrial relations; it is only recently, under the pressure of events, that the Institute has decided to intervene more noticeably through its advice, information, assistance and logistic support and, exceptionally, to take a stand on industrial redeployment. Nevertheless, the INI has not laid down uniform criteria. For example, the SEAT automobile company, which employs more than 25,000 persons and in which the INI is the majority shareholder, is quite free to pursue its long-standing practice of concluding agreements within the undertaking. SEAT is a member of the Spanish Association of Automobile Manufacturers; it is also affiliated to the CEOE but for information purposes only, as it is not covered by agreements concluded in the sector.

A survey conducted in 1982 [18] shows that bargaining in INI undertakings follows much the same pattern as in the private sector; 61 per cent of agreements concluded during that year were at the level of the undertaking, about the same as in the private sector. As far as their period of validity is concerned, 67 per cent of INI agreements were concluded for a period of one year and 23 per cent for two years, except as regards the economic clauses, indicating that the INI has a much stronger preference for one-year agreements than private undertakings. The stipulated structure of total wages is as follows: 43 per cent direct remuneration, 25 per cent wage increments, 2 per cent overtime, 23 per cent social security costs, and the remainder other social benefits.

It was not an easy task to determine whether the ceiling on wage increases (6.5 per cent) established for 1984 by the General Budget Act was binding or merely indicative for negotiations to be conducted in 1984 by INI undertakings. Many of the undertakings covered by the Act are not controlled by the INI, and the ceiling fixed in the budget might at most be interpreted as an instruction from the holding group to heads of undertakings whom the INI is in a position to appoint and to dismiss; at the same time, the abolition of the registration procedure has deprived the Government of the legal means to render null and void those agreements which exceed the established ceiling.

The fact that the wage increase rates for the public service laid down in the National Employment Agreement also applied to state public service undertakings was the result of an explicit agreement between the Government and the signatory trade union confederations; a large number of persons questioned maintained that this binding agreement did not apply to the 1984 negotiations and that the application of the wage ceiling was in fact merely one subject for negotiation among others and was not automatic, as in the case of the public service.

There was, however, no doubt that public service undertakings were subjected more strongly than others to detailed regulations and that their margin for negotiation was more often limited by programmes, investment plans and salary scales. The attitude of the negotiators could also vary according to whether the public service undertaking enjoyed a monopoly or not. Although negotiations were conducted by undertakings and not by the responsible ministry, they were influenced by the general and social situation prevailing at the time. There were cases, for example, where negotiations were held concurrently with the discussion of feasibility plans between the Government and the undertaking concerned.

The case of RENFE illustrates the extent and complexity of the problems that limit the State's decision-taking powers. It was intended under the contractual programme established by the Government in 1984, among other matters, to shorten the railway network, reduce staff, increase productivity by 16 per cent, modernise equipment and improve management. These objectives had a direct and indirect impact on the negotiations that were due to begin shortly after the visit by the mission, as the negotiators also had to disentangle the web of legal provisions, internal regulations, instructions and circulars still in force (RENFE's code of labour standards alone comprised 449 articles).

In spite of everything, the negotiations proceeded without acrimony and in an atmosphere of mutual respect. On the employers' side, the negotiations were conducted by the General Directorate of Personnel, which is composed of an Industrial Relations Division and a Personnel Administration Division (recruitment, advancement, etc.). The national railways comprise 134 establishments in each of which there is a works committee, with a general inter-establishment committee for the entire network. The latter committee's delegation to the negotiations was composed of members of four different unions (the CCOO, UGT, USO and the Railmen's Free Trade Union). Previously, the most difficult issues for negotiation had been social rights (guarantees and facilities) and job classification, but in 1984 protection of real wages and security of employment were to the fore. Moreover, a number of strikes, which on two occasions compelled the partners to have recourse to arbitration, have served as a reminder, if a reminder were necessary, of the difficulty of concluding a single agreement covering such a large number of employees. At all events, the RENFE agreement for 1984 could not in future be expected to serve as a basis for other negotiations, as was the case for the previous agreements.

The powers of the administrative authority are even more manifest in determining minimum essential services. In the national railways, for example, a Royal Degree of 1980, with accompanying circulars, establishes minimum staffing levels for this public service to operate. As was seen in the previous chapter, similar provisions apply to air and maritime transport, hospitals, ports, electricity and so on. Such minimum levels are always higher in public service undertakings than in undertakings in the INI group or the private sector;

similarly, their effects are felt more strongly in the event of non-observance or a strike. In fact, the question of dismissal and suspension of wages in the case of workers who fail to comply with the decrees on essential services has become a new issue for negotiation which is often the subject of acrimonious debate and complicates efforts to reach solutions.

Notes

[1] The XXXIIIrd Congress of the UGT in 1983 considered the question of independent trade unions in the public service and, after having referred to the causes of this phenomenon, expressed the hope that the major union movements, through their bargaining power and through flexible and liberal programmes, would swiftly attract the majority of workers currently affiliated to the independent unions. See UGT: *Resoluciones del XXXIII Congreso Confederal* (Madrid, June 1983), pp. 39 and 40.

[2] The Police Union, for example, claims a membership of 60 per cent of the police force.

[3] J. A. Sagardoy and D. León Blanco: *El poder sindical en España* (Madrid, Editorial Planeta, 1982), p. 103.

[4] As regards local officials, see, for example, the resolution of the General Directorate of Local Authorities (Ministry of Territorial Administration) of 29 January 1981.

[5] The Labour Relations (Public Service) Convention, 1978 (No. 151), does not deal with strikes by public employees.

[6] Tomás Sala Franco: "Prólogo", in J. López Gandia: *Los acuerdos colectivos en la relación de empleo público* (Models of Comparative Law) (Madrid, Instituto de Estudios Sociales, 1981), p. 10.

[7] Antonio Ojeda Avilés: *Derecho sindical* (Madrid, Editorial Tecnos, 1980), p. 387.

[8] See ILO: *Freedom of association and collective bargaining: General survey by the Committee of Experts on the Application of Conventions and Recommendations* (Geneva, 1983), para. 214.

[9] FETAP is a federation of public employees' unions affiliated to the UGT; it is now called the Federation of Public Services (FSP).

[10] The full text of this agreement is given in Luis Enrique de la Villa: *Panorama de las relaciones laborales en España* (Madrid, Editorial Tecnos, 1983) p. 210.

[11] FSP Executive Committee: *Acuerdo sobre retribuciones del personal al servicio del Estado y sus organismos autónomes para el ejercicio de 1983* (mimeographed), p. 1.

[12] *Gaceta Sindical* (Madrid, CCOO), No. 3, p. 27.

[13] Paragraph 6 of the preamble to the Bill on freedom of association.

[14] This recognition has, however, only been accorded for the specific purposes of wage review.

[15] According to the report of the National Institute of Industries (INI), only six of the undertakings in the INI group employed less than 100 workers. See INI: *La negociación colectiva en 1982 del Grupo INI* (Madrid, 1981), pp. 18-20.

[16] Ministry of Economy and Finance, General Directorate of Economic Policy: *La negociación colectiva en 1982. Principales características económicas y tendencias* (Madrid, Publicaciones de la Secretaría General Técnica, 1983), p. 40.

[17] *Gaceta Sindical*, Year IV, No. 25, p. 10.

[18] INI: *La negociación colectiva en 1982 del Grupo INI*, op. cit., pp. 21 and 22.

FINAL REMARKS

9

In 1969, when the Study Group entrusted by the Governing Body of the ILO with examining trade union and labour problems in Spain presented its report, the system prevailing in the country was a corporative one in which association was compulsory. Since then, the relations between employers' associations, trade union organisations and the public authorities have been drastically changed by the new Constitution and by copious legislation. These texts guarantee many freedoms, among them freedom of association in occupational organisations; the latter have been endowed with the means necessary to defend and promote the interests of their members, in particular the freedom to negotiate conditions of employment and the possibility, where necessary, of resorting to forms of pressure such as strikes or, within certain limits, lock-outs.

But this rapid evolution has not taken place without a certain amount of trial and error, not to say friction, and some gaps still remain. As we have seen, instances of trial and error have been found in defining the respective roles of union representatives and autonomous forms of workers' representation within the undertaking, which have been marked by overlapping between the powers of the former and the competence of the latter. They were also revealed by the mission's analysis of the role of the State or autonomous communities in negotiating collective agreements at a higher level.

Instances of friction and erratic progress have also been mentioned in several parts of this report. Thus it has referred to the often bitter rivalries between the various trends within the trade union movement. The devolution of the trade union assets of the former corporative organisation is beyond doubt a major bone of contention among the various confederations. Under the former Government it underlay all calculations, fuelled all suspicions and animated all conversations in the circles concerned, and it continues to do so under the new one. Of course this may easily be explained by the sums of money involved; meanwhile, all are agreed on the urgency — not to mention the difficulty — of finding a solution.

Finally, the mission has been very frank in reporting on the gaps in the present system of industrial relations in the country that were pointed out to it by informed observers.

First of all, there is the absence of effective conciliation, mediation and voluntary arbitration procedures for resolving collective labour disputes. Improvements in these procedures do not necessarily require the adoption of a law; they may also result from an agreement between employers' associations and trade unions. What is important is that this gap should be filled without delay. Next, there is the uncertainty in the public service as to the possibility of determining conditions of employment by collective bargaining or other forms of participation, and as regards the right to strike. Here again, as the people to whom the mission spoke fully realised, some clarification would appear necessary. The ratification by Spain of the ILO Labour Relations (Public Service) Convention, 1978 (No. 151), should make it possible to find a speedier solution to these problems.

Such difficulties as these are only to be expected when a country changes drastically the structure of its collective labour relations, and indeed some observers predicted that the difficulties would become even greater. The most remarkable thing about the recent developments is that they have not provoked greater shocks or upheavals.

In the field with which we are concerned, the mission is convinced that the changes taking place are the result of a concerted effort by the public authorities and the employers' and workers' organisations to find universally acceptable solutions to the innumerable problems, both past and present, with which they have been faced. Its members were impressed by the competence of the senior officials whom they met, by the sense of dialogue and the readiness to seek jointly agreed solutions displayed by most of the employers and union leaders they visited, and by the concern shown by all the persons they encountered to respect the basic human freedoms, without which the rights of employers' associations and trade union organisations would remain a dead letter.

All this cannot but be favourable to the progress of this delicate phase of the history of Spain, a progress which its citizens view on the whole as harmonious. It also bodes well for future developments in the country.

APPENDICES

APPENDICES

Working Party on the Trade Union Situation and Labour Relations Systems in European Countries: Report of the meeting held on 5 November 1984

1. The Working Party was established by the Governing Body at its 227th (June 1984) Session to discuss the studies on the trade union situation and industrial relations systems in Spain and Yugoslavia.

2. The Working Party was composed of the following:

Government group:	Miss Dimond (United Kingdom)
	Mr. Heldal (Norway)
	Mr. Oudovenko (Ukrainian SSR)
Employers' group:	Mr. Decosterd
	Miss Hak
	Mr. Rowe
Workers' group:	Mr. Mehta
	Mr. Svenningsen

3. At the same session, the Governing Body had decided to invite Spain and Yugoslavia to designate one person each from government, employers' and workers' circles to be represented at the Working Party, to keep the two studies confidential until the Working Party had completed its discussions and to instruct the Working Party to report to the Governing Body at its 228th (November 1984), or 229th (February-March 1985) Session.

4. The Working Party elected Mr. Heldal, Government member (Norway), as its Chairman.

5. Opening the meeting, Mr. Bolin, Deputy Director-General of the ILO, recalled that, in January 1974, the Second European Regional Conference — in a unanimous resolution on freedom of association and industrial relations in Europe — had called for studies "analysing in the most exhaustive manner possible the trade union situation and industrial relations existing within the framework of the various economic and social systems of the European countries in the light of the international standards adopted by the ILO in this field, as well as the experience acquired and data collected by the competent ILO bodies". The resolution had recommended that "these studies should provide a basis, at a future session of the European Regional Conference or a meeting specially convened for the purpose, for a wide exchange of views and experiences and for a frank and objective confrontation of ideas with a view to achieving better knowledge and understanding". The Third European Regional Conference (October 1979), in a resolution, also adopted unanimously, on freedom of association, trade union rights and industrial relations in Europe, invited the Governing Body to implement this recommendation. It was

consequently proposed to make provision in the budget of the Organisation for a series of country studies on the trade union situation and industrial relations systems in Europe. These proposals were adopted by the International Labour Conference. The first two studies, on Hungary and Norway, were considered by a Working Party in November 1983 and by the Governing Body at its session in February-March 1984.

6. Mr. Bolin stressed that these studies could not in any way be regarded as a substitute for the procedures for supervising the application of international labour Conventions. That had already been emphasised in the Governing Body during the discussion on the first two studies. However, the ILO also had as its task the collection of all available information on matters within its competence. Here it had done so on a matter — relations between managements, workers organised into trade unions and other bodies, and public authorities, and more particularly freedom of association — which was naturally a major subject for analysis, reflection and discussion in an organisation wholly concerned with labour problems. Missions had gone to Spain and Yugoslavia, and he wished to thank the two Governments for having agreed to such an analysis being made in the case of their countries. In both Spain and Yugoslavia, the authors of the studies had met representatives of governments, of enterprises and of the trade union movements, as well as judicial and academic personalities, whom they had asked whatever questions they thought fit. On returning to Geneva, they had digested the mass of information gathered, drafted the studies and tried to convey a picture of the trade union situation and industrial relations systems in Spain and Yugoslavia, in the light of the relevant standards of the ILO. Once the draft studies had been completed, they had been sent to the governments concerned, well before the present meeting, so as to enable them to inform the authors of any errors or inaccuracies they might contain. Although the information thus received had been duly taken into account, naturally it was the authors who assumed responsibility for the findings and final assessments in the studies; they alone were responsible for the final text.

7. Mr. Mehta, speaking on behalf of the Worker members, expressed the view that the principles which had been established the year before for discussion of the studies on Hungary and Norway by a working party should be followed in the case of the two present studies. In particular, the same rules of procedure should apply: the authors bore responsibility for the findings and assessments in these studies, which were not a substitute for ILO supervisory procedures. The members of the Working Party should not call into question the substance of the studies but, if necessary, should ask for the correction of technical errors or seek clarifications. He complimented the Office on the quality of the new studies, adding that the Worker members would like them to be published.

8. Miss Hak, speaking on behalf of the Employer members, welcomed the publication of the first two studies, on Hungary and Norway, and expressed the conviction that they, along with the two new studies, would be highly appreciated. She was grateful to the ILO for the work it had done and much appreciated the studies on Spain and Yugoslavia, which, of course, remained the responsibility of their authors. The Working Party's report should be approved, in accordance with a written procedure, by the members and attached to the studies for submission to the Governing Body.

9. The Chairman noted that the members of the Working Party were in agreement on applying the principles and procedure of the year before. The discussion would deal first with the trade union situation and industrial relations system in Spain, and then with those of Yugoslavia.

10. Professor Jaime Montalvo Correa, representative of the Spanish Government, conveyed the thanks and congratulations of his Government on the study undertaken by the ILO. Spain had always accorded the highest importance to social questions and was particularly sympathetic to the work of the ILO. His country's interest had grown since the restoration of democracy. The 1968 report of the ILO Study Group, published in 1969,

had been of exceptional importance for all who were then working for the recovery of trade union freedoms. The report of the 1983 mission described some of the profound changes which had occurred between 1969 and 1983 and which, for the Government and people of Spain, were matters of the greatest satisfaction. They were reflected in the Constitution of 1978 which enshrined the rights of assembly, association and participation, as well as freedom to organise and the right to strike, which were "super-protected" rights in the sense that they were to be defined by a fundamental law which must be adopted by an absolute majority of the Cortes. Any natural or juridical person could defend his or its rights by an appeal directly to the Constitutional Court.

11. His Government appreciated the very high standard of the ILO report. It brought out the great successes as well as the principal shortcomings of the Spanish system of industrial relations. The report rightly pointed out that the change in labour relations was very largely due to the combined efforts of the Government and the social partners. On the other hand, it drew attention to certain problems, chief among them the absence in Spain of an appropriate procedure for settling conflicts of interest.

12. Professor Montalvo then pointed out some technical errors in the report and suggested corrections, which were duly noted by the secretariat. He also presented the observations and remarks of his Government regarding some matters of substance examined in the report. Lastly, he provided some additional information and drew attention to certain important events which had occurred in Spain after the mission's visit.

13. The Government pointed out that Article 149.1.7 of the Spanish Constitution established the exclusive competence of the State regarding labour legislation, in relation to both laws and regulations, and in accordance, moreover, with judgements handed down on a number of occasions by the Constitutional Court (S 4 May, 14 June and 30 June 1982, inter alia), whereby such a transfer (which would also take place through the fundamental legislation on social security) would be contrary to the express provisions of the Constitution on this matter and to the guiding principles of equality and non-discrimination, solidarity, elimination of privileges, and freedom of movement and residence; by contrast, the Government observed that in the administration and application of labour legislation the Autonomous Communities enjoyed extensive powers by virtue of their having replaced the State Administration, an important transfer of powers having occurred in many cases. Moreover, it would hamper state planning of the economy, which was also governed by the Constitution. On a practical level, the transfer of legislative powers pertaining to labour and social security would be prejudicial to the economic principle of a single market. Similarly, the transfer of powers in the field of trade union legislation would also be contrary to the Constitution, which laid down that freedom of association must be regulated by a fundamental law, a matter reserved to the Cortes.

14. Several paragraphs of the report dealt with the reduction of working hours. His Government wished to point out that, between 1976 and 1979, the latter had declined at the rate of 30 hours per year, and by 50 hours since then. Prior to the signature of the Inter-Confederation Framework Agreement (AMI) of 1980, statutory working hours had been 2,006 per year; in 1984 the figure was 1,826 hours and 27 minutes, as required by Act No. 4 of 1983.

15. The report also referred to the "special systems" provided for by the Workers' Charter. The Government wished to supplement that information by indicating that a recent law (Act No. 32 of 1984) had the labour relations of dockworkers added to the list of special systems.

16. The Spanish Government had a number of objections to certain remarks in the report; for example it was not entirely in agreement with the report's assessment that "there is quite a strong politicisation in the relationships between workers and employers"

(Chapter 2). The safeguards established by the Workers' Charter had been intended for the bodies responsible for the collective representation of the workforce, i.e. works committees and staff representatives, and not specifically for trade union representatives. On the question of anti-union practices, he thought it appropriate to add that the law provided for appeals procedures, even to the Constitutional Court, in case of anti-union discrimination. As a matter of fact, the Court had repeatedly heard cases dealing with that question and had decided that dismissals motivated by discriminatory anti-union practices were automatically null and void. Furthermore, the Fundamental Law on Freedom of Association (LOLS), which was passed by the Cortes on 16 July 1984 but which had not yet entered into force because of an appeal pending before the Constitutional Court filed by a number of opposition political groups and the Basque legislature, introduced a series of protective measures inspired by ILO Conventions Nos. 98 and 135, as well as by the jurisprudence of the Spanish courts and in particular the Constitutional Court.

17. As to the representative character of employers' associations, his Government considered that the estimates in the report — for example, that the Spanish Confederation of Employers' Organisations (CEOE) represented "over 1,300,000 undertakings" — were exaggerated; in any case, a large share of the CEOE's representativity was accounted for by its affiliate, the Confederation of Small and Medium-Sized Undertakings (CEPYME), although these organisations undeniably represented a large majority.

18. The report also touched on the question of "solidarity contributions" under collective agreements. That question had never been ruled upon by the Constitutional Court. As to the Central Labour Court (TCT), it had had occasion to rule on this question in connection with cases brought by individuals. In these, it had stated that such contributions could not be required because they had no legal basis. The TCT had considered that solidarity contributions were a matter which lay at the very core of freedom of association and, under the Constitution, must consequently be regulated by a fundamental law. It should be added that the Fundamental Law on Freedom of Association (which, as already indicated, had not yet entered into force) contained provisions which made solidarity contributions valid provided the individual worker concerned gave notice in writing of his consent, in accordance with procedures to be specified in the relevant collective agreement.

19. The report also referred to the role of the State in wage negotiations. The Government wished to point out that the State, without interfering directly, nevertheless had a policy of closely following wage discussions between the social partners. That role had been apparent, for example, in the negotiation of the economic and social agreement of October 1984 (see below). Moreover, in the collective bargaining that took place in 1984, the State had, in the relevant financial legislation, set a ceiling of 6.5 per cent for wage increases in the civil service and state enterprises, and had suggested, as a guide, the same ceiling for negotiations in the private sector.

20. He wondered whether it was not a fact that, as the law now stood, a trade union's request for registration could be suspended or even rejected. He also stated that the term "legal representatives" used in the law implementing the Workers' Charter could not apply, strictly speaking, to union representatives (Chapter 3 of the report). He was also of the opinion that the clashes between the police and strikers, which in the past had led to complaints to the Committee on Freedom of Association, had caused fewer deaths among workers than the report indicated (Chapter 4).

21. In concluding his statement, Professor Montalvo informed the Working Party of the main developments that had occurred in Spanish labour law and relations during 1984:

(1) The *Fundamental Law on Freedom of Association (LOLS) (see also above)*: The law in question recognised the right to join a trade union, both in the private sector and in the public administration, subject to a few exceptions: the armed forces, members of the

judiciary and state prosecutors (without prejudice to their right of association, subject to special rules); special conditions could be established to regulate the rights of the state security bodies and forces. The *content* of freedom of association, under the LOLS, was, he said, consistent with the principles of ILO Conventions Nos. 87 and 98, ratified by Spain. Self-employed workers, and unemployed and retired persons could not, however, form separate trade unions but they could join existing unions. The State could not interfere in the internal affairs of organisations; its involvement was limited to the registration of unions and the filing of their statutes, without prejudice to the right of the courts to intervene in defence of legality. A trade union could be suspended or dissolved only by virtue of a final court decision based on *serious* non-compliance with the law. (The question of solidarity contributions had already been referred to.) The law accepted trade union pluralism but conferred certain prerogatives on the most representative trade unions and established a "graduated" criterion for assessing their representative character, i.e. in terms of support (measured by the number of votes) but also in accordance with the representative character of the national trade union or autonomous community to which the lower-level union was affiliated. Lastly, the most representative trade unions nation-wide or at the level of the autonomous community enjoyed certain privileges: they could sign national (or autonomous community) agreements and be represented on the executive bodies of certain institutions in which provision was made for participation by employers' and workers' organisations.

(2) *Developments in collective bargaining in 1984.* As indicated in the report, the social partners had not been able to conclude a framework agreement during the early months of 1984. Nevertheless, collective bargaining had not encountered too many difficulties. As a matter of fact, the increase in the proportion of disputes as compared with 1983 must be attributed to problems connected with industrial restructuring rather than to collective bargaining. Although the final results of collective bargaining for 1984 could as yet not be determined, according to the Ministry of Labour wage increases were in the neighbourhood of 7.9 per cent, i.e. very close to the claim put forward by the UGT at the beginning of the year.

(3) *The Economic and Social Agreement (AES).* This agreement was signed on 9 October 1984 by the CEOE and the CEPYME for the employers, the UGT for the trade unions, and the Government, which meant that the social partners and the Government had returned to the concept of tripartite agreement. The AES was due to remain in force until 1986. It was divided into three parts. The first consisted of a statement by the Government, signed by the Prime Minister. The commitments entered into by the parties were then set forth under two headings: Title I comprised the commitments of the State as well as the tripartite commitments. It declared that the promotion of employment was the priority objective of the Government's policy. To that end, a number of measures were envisaged, namely tax incentives to investment, labour-intensive public works, increased subsidies to the National Employment Institute with a view to the conclusion of agreements for schemes creating employment for 160,000-190,000 jobseekers, the establishment of a Solidarity Fund (managed by a tripartite body) to carry out programmes similar to those of the European Social Fund, and the reduction of employer contributions to social security. Other commitments comprised the appointment of a tripartite commission on social security reform. Still others related to safety and health as well as to participation. It was provided, for example, that the State would negotiate with the trade union which had signed the AES on the question of improving trade union rights in public enterprises. Title I also dealt with hiring and vocational training, and particularly with the harmonisation of Spain's labour legislation with that of the European Economic Community. To that end, the organisations signing the agreement would establish a commission to draw up and submit appropriate proposals to the Government. Title II of the AES consisted of bilateral commitments and incorporated certain solutions and certain techniques which had been applied in connection with earlier inter-occupational negotiations. In the matter of wages, it provided that the increases to be negotiated in 1985

would fall within a bracket ranging from a minimum of 5.5 per cent to a maximum of 7.5 per cent. For 1986, they would have as their point of reference the rate of inflation anticipated by the Government for that year and would fall within a bracket ranging between a minimum of 90 per cent of that inflation and a maximum of 107 per cent. Wage changes would be possible if real inflation exceeded the estimates, and "release" clauses were envisaged for enterprises in economic difficulty. Title II also included measures to encourage productivity and discourage absenteeism, double jobbing and overtime working. It also included criteria for co-ordinating or dovetailing the various stages of collective bargaining in the interests of efficiency, and it provided for the establishment of a joint inter-confederation committee to interpret and supervise its operation. It contained an article designed to promote the linkage of collective agreements. The AES also dealt with certain problems mentioned in the report: article 22 contained a commitment by the Government to prepare and submit to the Cortes, within six months and after consultation with the most representative trade union and employers' organisations, a draft law on the distribution of "accumulated" trade union assets. In the matter of settlement of collective labour disputes, it recorded a commitment by the signatory organisations to negotiate by 31 December 1986 a specific inter-confederation agreement on voluntary dispute settlement procedures, possibly taking account of the principles of the ILO Voluntary Conciliation and Arbitration Recommendation (No. 92) and of article 6 of the European Social Charter. Among those principles, mention should be made of simplicity and rapidity of procedure, the voluntary character of mediation and arbitration in all but exceptional cases, and the free choice of mediators and arbitrators (on the latter point it was perhaps worth adding that the Labour Relations Board of the Basque country had already drafted and adopted a model agreement on mediation, conciliation and arbitration in the course of 1984. However, because of the problems of transfer of powers mentioned previously, there were doubts concerning its legal effectiveness).

22. Mr. J. M. Lacasa Aso, representative of the Spanish employers, thanked the members of the ILO mission for their work in Spain, and asked the Office to convey special congratulations from the CEOE to the head of the mission, Mr. Efrén Córdova, who had recently retired. The report had been read with great interest at the CEOE, and the employers considered it comprehensive and objective. That did not mean, of course, that they were always and necessarily in agreement with all the observations in it. For example, the report mentioned certain anti-union practices, which in the opinion of the CEOE did not exist, but which, if they had happened, had occurred in the public sector.

23. The Spanish employers also wished to stress their commitment to the policy of co-operation. The Economic and Social Agreement of 1984 was only an extension of that policy. Among the undertakings entered into in that agreement by the parties, mention should be made of the commitment to work towards the alignment of Spain's labour legislation with that of the EEC, particularly as regards collective dismissals, regarding which Spanish legislation is extremely strict by comparison with the usual practice in most other EEC countries, and also of the commitment to prepare an instrument on the settlement of labour disputes. Mr. Lacasa Aso also requested the Working Party to take note of the fact that the entry into force of the Fundamental Law on Freedom of Association, which had been mentioned several times by the representative of the Spanish Government, had been suspended owing to the filing of an appeal with the Constitutional Court (see above).

24. In view of the CEOE, the Economic and Social Agreement covered three basic areas.

The first concerned the Government's statement of economic policy, endorsed by the President of the CEOE, which brought together a number of agreements and objectives affecting the macro-economy, which, however, had an extremely serious impact on the operations of undertakings and on their competitiveness, and consequently on the possibilities of job creation. It naturally covered fiscal pressure, the public sector deficit, inflation forecasts, the fall in interest rates, incomes policy, the reform of public undertakings and industrial policy aimed at overcoming the obsolescence of certain sectors and improving our means of production.

Secondly, it comprised a number of agreements and tripartite settlements concluded between the Government, the General Union of Workers (UGT), CEPYME and CEOE. These agreements were of various types: they concerned tax incentives for investment and economic measures to promote investment and to further various types of activity intended to promote vocational training and innovation and to compensate for a number of regional imbalances regarding unemployment benefits, occupational safety and health, social security contributions and the reform of social security, as well as the labour market, including the conclusion and termination of the employment relationship and other aspects resulting in the establishment of a number of committees to discuss structural reform to make the system more flexible and to improve Spain's capacity to adapt to the new geographical and economic context that she was about to enter, the European Economic Community.

The third area consisted of settlements affecting the collective bargaining process in all agreements to be concluded in Spain during the 1985-86 period. As was normal in industrial relations in the narrow sense, this package deal was naturally entered into only by CEPYME, CEOE and the General Union of Workers (UGT) and constituted an inter-confederal agreement, treated in accordance with applicable Spanish standards. It covered the margin within which collective bargaining on wage increases would take place in Spain in 1985 and 1986, and included provision for such bargaining to range between 5.5 and 7.5 per cent in 1985, and between 5.4 and 6.8 per cent in 1986. Account should be taken of the government forecast for inflation in 1985, set at 7.0 per cent; it was forecast that this would fall to 6.0 per cent in 1986.

Other aspects of this inter-confederal agreement concerned the promotion of productivity and the reduction of absenteeism, occupational safety and health, bargaining structures, voluntary procedures for the settlement of disputes in line with international labour Recommendation No. 92 and the duration of validity of agreements.

25. Mr. Santillán Cabeza, a Spanish workers' representative, stated that the report was a very important source of information about the Spanish trade union situation. There were some matters, however, on which the General Union of Workers (UGT) disagreed with it, either because it did not share the approach or because it considered that the report did not mention or did not give sufficient attention to certain very important questions. For example, the report did not sufficiently emphasise the very severe repression which the trade unions had suffered during the dictatorship. That was a very painful matter for all Spaniards. While it was true that Spaniards now wish to build their democracy with their eyes on the future, that was no reason why they should forget the past. On the question of anti-union practices, it could be said that they were not very frequent in Spain and not more frequent in Catalonia than elsewhere. As to the role of the workers' assemblies in collective bargaining (Chapter 5 of the report), it was true that *information* meetings were frequent, but assemblies held for the purpose of taking decisions were now much less so. On the question of hours of work, most court decisions on the application of the 40-hour law had, as a matter of fact, been favourable to the workers. Lastly, the report should have given more attention to the very important role played by the Constitutional Court in the adaptation of trade union legislation to the democratic principles of the 1978 Constitution.

26. Nor could the UGT entirely subscribe to the report's closing remarks. In its opinion, the major bone of contention among the various trade union confederations was not the question of the devolution of trade union assets but ideological differences.

27. He added that, unlike certain other central trade union organisations, the UGT had always been in favour of co-operation. It attached a great importance to the economic and social agreement, which it considered very constructive. The agreement strengthened the participation of social organisations in certain state institutions.

28. Miss Dimond, Government member (United Kingdom), said that she had found the report very interesting and thanked all who had taken part in its preparation. She sought some additional explanations on certain points, such as trade union elections, the financing of trade unions in Spain and labour disputes.

29. Professor Montalvo, in reply, explained that in Spain "trade union elections" were actually, as indicated in the report, elections of workers' delegates and members of works committees. As to financing, it was accepted in his country that the Government should pay subsidies to the trade unions and employers' associations. These subsidies were, however, not large and the main source of trade unions funds was still, and by far, the dues paid by their members. The reason why the State paid such subsidies was that employers' and workers' organisations were considered to be something more than private associations (as in the nineteenth century) because the Constitution recognised that they played a role in the institutional functioning of the country. If it was accepted that the State could pay subsidies to political parties, it could also be accepted that it could pay subsidies to employers' and workers' organisations. On the question of labour disputes, Professor Montalvo added that the right to strike was recognised by the Constitution in terms that ranked it even above the right to work and therefore certain measures, such as the organisation of strike pickets, were perfectly legal provided they were peaceful. At the moment, there was a certain amount of social tension due to industrial restructuring, which explained the relatively high number of labour disputes. The Government was now working on a draft law concerning strikes.

30. Mr. Oudovenko, Government member (Ukrainian SSR), considered the report very interesting because it presented a fairly comprehensive picture of the trade union and labour relations situation in Spain. It showed what had been done in the country in recent years and highlighted the progress that had been made, especially in view of the heavy burden of the past. Nevertheless, the report did not sufficiently emphasise certain crucial problems, such as the very high rate of unemployment, the economic crisis and inflation. Nor did it pay sufficient attention to the role of the trade unions in the discussion and solution of those problems and in the improvement of employment and working conditions.

31. Miss Hak, Employer member (Netherlands), also considered the report excellent. She stressed the importance of clearly indicating that the Fundamental Law on Freedom of Association had not as yet entered into force.

32. Mr. Mehta, Worker member (India), also associated himself with the congratulations of other members concerning the report. He added that the Committee on Freedom of Association had not received any complaint concerning the draft Fundamental Law on Freedom of Association, which meant that it was not contrary to ILO standards and principles.

33. Speaking on the study dealing with her country, Miss Ilic, representative of the Government of Yugoslavia, stressed the importance attached by her country to trade union rights and said that the efforts of the mission to understand the specific characteristics of its economic and social system and to describe the overall situation in an objective manner had been highly appreciated. She paid tribute to the memory of Mr. Lagergren who had headed the mission, and thanked Mr. Servais for having come to Belgrade to discuss certain questions during the final stage of the report and to make the necessary corrections on certain factual and legal matters. The Yugoslav Government considered the report to be objective. It wished to emphasise, however, that the specific nature of the system and its special terminology had led to a lack of precision on certain points, particularly on relations between the Confederation of Trade Unions and the League of Communists, which had been somewhat oversimplified, and on relations between the Government and the Confederation of Trade Unions.

34. She pointed out that, in the section devoted to the relations of the trade union movement with the Government, the report referred specifically and exclusively to the Confederation of Trade Unions in connection with certain functions at the federal level, e.g. the right to sign certain social or self-management agreements, to express opinions on draft laws in the field of analysis, planning, statistical information and other indicators of the results of workers' activities, and the performance of base organisations and of other bodies in connection with management of income and economic activities based on social resources. That was due to the fact that the Confederation was the only trade union organisation at the federal level. Nevertheless, in the laws cited in the report and in particular in the law on associated work, mention was made of trade unions in numerous articles without referring to the name of the trade union organisation at the federal level or at any other level. Lastly, she pointed out some technical errors that had slipped into the report.

35. Mr. Franić, the representative of Yugoslav workers, observed that in a situation characterised by prejudice, ignorance and sometimes even lack of any desire to understand systems other than those to which one was accustomed, such studies on the trade union situation and labour relations in European countries could, by their impartial analysis and the information they provided, help towards a better understanding of the trade union movement and thus greater co-operation in the European framework and even beyond it. After paying tribute to the mission for its efforts to arrive at the best possible understanding of the trade union situation in Yugoslavia, Mr. Franić recognised that the task was not an easy one and it was not surprising that the report should occasionally be ambiguous or imprecise. On the whole, however, the mission had carried out its task successfully.

36. He pointed out that owing to the fact that there were no employers in Yugoslavia in the usual meaning of the term, whether private individuals or the State, the traditional opposition between workers and employers did not exist. The two were merged and subject to the control of the associated workers. All matters concerning labour relations and negotiations involving a balance of strength in traditional models of industrial relations were, in Yugoslavia, decided by the workers themselves. The role of the trade unions was thus adapted to the exigencies of that system. The principles relating to that role and to the position of the trade unions were contained in Point VIII of the Preamble to the Federal Constitution, as mentioned in the report. In his view, the complete application of those principles signified the total liberation of labour and the introduction into the life of workers of the principle contained in the Declaration of Philadelphia that "labour is not a commodity". Point VIII of the Federal Constitution made it clear that the task of the trade unions was to struggle for the direct interests of workers, for the improvement of their social and material status, and therefore for the objectives which traditionally motivated trade union action.

37. On the subject of relations between the trade union movement and the League of Communists, he stressed some instances of imprecision in the report which, in his view, were probably due to the fact that certain aspects of Yugoslav development might have been too difficult to grasp by the mission in so short a time, especially as it was hard to escape the influence of stereotypes. Instead of citing facts, the report used such expressions as "we were told", which he felt should have been more precise and have referred to facts; it would have been preferable for the analysis to have been made on the basis of original documents. Thus with regard to the relations between the trade unions, on the one hand, and the political party and the Government, on the other, the following facts should have been explicitly mentioned. First of all, neither the Yugoslav Constitution nor Yugoslav legislation contained any provision requiring the trade unions to execute the directives of the Government, of a political party or of any other body outside the trade unions. He emphasised that, for that reason, the ILO Committee of Experts on the Application of Conventions and Recommendations had not had occasion to express any comments on

the subject. Secondly, neither did the rules of the Confederation of Trade Unions or the League of Communists or of other institutions contain any provision requiring the trade unions to carry out decisions taken by non-trade union organs. Thirdly, there was no political theory in the country involving a transmission-belt role to be played by the trade unions on behalf of the State or a political party. Lastly, Yugoslav political theory, including the official ideological and theoretical guide-lines of the League of Communists, firmly supported the position that trade unions could not carry out their functions unless they enjoyed independence and freedom in their activities.

38. Illustrating the way in which this issue was dealt with in the Yugoslav political theory, he quoted the well-known Yugoslav theoretician, Eduard Kardelj, who had written that the trade unions were certainly right in saying that they should not assume responsibilities for decisions of government decision-making bodies, which on their part would not always be able to comply with the demands of trade unions. Eduard Kardelj had further added that to underestimate the protective role of trade unions or to limit their freedom to exercise their role would be highly detrimental to the self-management system. If the trade union played that role in the Yugoslav socio-economic system, society must enable it to carry out that role in the political system as well. Since, under the Constitution, the trade union had been incorporated in the system of management of associated work, it must also be included in the political system. The leading organs of the trade unions must not confine themselves to determining overall policy and general lines of action; they must propose their solutions to the political institutions and make sure that they were implemented. Such a political basis for developing the role of the trade unions, the speaker continued, did not have much in common with the idea that trade unions could or should be the executors of policies adopted by other organs. If the trade unions failed to carry out their tasks successfully, that would be due not to their position in the socio-political system of the country but to their own weaknesses. The authors of the report had rightly pointed out that the objective of Yugoslav policy was to ensure "the active participation of all the people in the decision-making machinery in the political, social and economic fields". In that case, it was unthinkable for any political power or party to be able to have a monopoly of decision-making. Self-management excluded monopoly in the decision-making process and vice versa.

39. He thought it necessary to clarify certain points, which he considered vague or one-sided, dealing with the position of the party because relations between trade unions and parties were questions of capital importance in all countries. It was natural for trade unions to take their own decisions concerning their relations with political parties and for them to be close to the party which most strongly supported their objectives and claims. In that respect, he observed, Yugoslavs found the experience of other countries interesting. He regretted that the study on Norway had not given more space to that subject since, from the short paragraph dealing with it, it was easy to see that there were very close relations between the trade union and the party and that the experience of mutual co-operation had been satisfactory.

40. He then mentioned some errors in the text of the report. He stressed that there were lessons to be drawn from the four studies, which should not be the last and, in particular, uniform criteria should be established to assist understanding of the various aspects of industrial relations, irrespective of the country or system concerned. Before completing his statements, the workers' representative honoured the memory of Mr. Lagergren for having done his utmost to give a faithful description in the report of the trade union situation and labour relations in Yugoslavia. He then referred to the important role and personal contribution of the other members of the mission in the preparation of the report and expressed to them his gratitude and that of his colleagues. He extended his thanks to the mission for having succeeded by a great effort in making the complexity of the Yugoslav system understandable to foreign readers and thereby making it accessible to those who were interested in the experiences of the Yugoslav workers.

41. Miss Dimond, Government member (United Kingdom), laid stress on the quality of the report. She emphasised the complexity of the system and in particular the difficulty of understanding certain aspects of self-management, which was a relatively new concept. She wondered whether this did not have an influence on the degree of support ordinary trade union members gave to their trade union. One of the functions of the trade union was, according to the report, to ensure that self-management functioned efficiently, and she wondered how that happened in practice. She also asked about the links between the policy of extensive decentralisation and self-management. Lastly, she asked for clarification concerning the situation in agriculture, in particular on the way in which that sector was integrated into the economy as a whole.

42. Mr. Svenningsen, Worker member (Denmark), asked about the reasons which had led Yugoslavia to withdraw from the International Labour Organisation in 1949 and to return in 1951. He also inquired about the complaint which had been made to the Committee on Freedom of Association in 1958.

43. In reply to the concerns expressed by Miss Dimond, Mr. Franić said that there was no doubt that the system was complex and it might appear complicated, especially to foreigners who met with it for the first time. However, for Yugoslavs who had lived with it from the early stages of its development, it was not so. Naturally, it was not an easy task to develop the participation of millions of people in decision-making, taking particularly into consideration that pre-war Yugoslavia was a backward country, without a working class with an industrial tradition, with a high rate of illiteracy, with considerable regional disparities in terms of development and so on. Noting that it took two centuries for the West to develop the present-day parliamentary democracy and industrial relations, he pointed out that the system installed in his country was recent and needed some time to be fully developed to function smoothly. Self-management was not a static model for all time — it must be regarded as an evolving system designed to encourage the maximum participation by all. It was the operation of the system in practice that determined what modifications might be needed. Within that framework, it was the task of the trade unions to create the best conditions (in housing, education, employment, etc.) for workers to exercise fully their self-management rights. As to decentralisation, in the Yugoslav context, its object was to enable everyone to make the greatest possible contribution to running the country's affairs. In so far as power was not exercised directly by the people, that objective could hardly be achieved. On the other hand, the system of workers' self-management could not function successfully if it were enclosed within the factory gates. It is for this reason that self-management had been extended, through delegations and delegates, to all the institutions in communes and further up in the province, republic and federation respectively.

44. Referring to agriculture, he pointed first to the existence of the part of agriculture organised within the so-called *Kombinats*, large agro-industrial complexes comprising farming, cattle-raising, food-processing and so on, in which the social and labour conditions were the same as in other sectors, and a private sector in which farmers had contractual relations with large agricultural undertakings or other contractual relations. The agricultural co-operatives facilitated the exchange of products between the farmers and the markets and provided other services to farmers, such as expert advice, seeds and so on. Farmers were now enjoying much better social protection — health care, pension insurance, etc. — which added increasingly to the reduction of differences in conditions of life in rural and urban areas. This was an important development in slowing down the migration from villages to towns. At the present moment, only 19.9 per cent of the Yugoslav active population remained in villages living on agriculture, as distinct from 1945 when more than 70 per cent of the population depended on agricultural production.

45. Mr. Servais, a member of the ILO mission, replied to Mr. Svenningsen's question concerning Yugoslavia's withdrawal from the ILO for a brief period between 1949 and

1951. For Yugoslavia, that was a period of social, economic and political transition. On the other question, he indicated that paragraphs 63 to 69 of the Thirtieth Report of the Committee on Freedom of Association dealt with the only case concerning Yugoslavia which that body had had to consider. The complaint has been made on 25 February 1958 by an international centre of free trade unionists in exile in Paris with regard to alleged prosecution of representatives of the trade union movement. The complaining organisation had subsequently informed the ILO, however, that it had not been its intention to file a formal complaint. Noting that the organisation could not have been induced to take that action by any kind of pressure since it was based in Paris, the Committee and the Governing Body had decided not to pursue the case.

46. Mr. Oudovenko, Government member (Ukrainian SSR), said that the report contained interesting information which showed the active role played by Yugoslav trade unions. He observed that the forms and activities of trade unions varied from country to country in keeping with the diversity of economic systems and methods. He referred to the proposal made at the 1984 Session of the International Labour Conference to hold a seminar on the situation and role of trade unions in the socialist countries. Nine central trade union organisations had joined in making the proposal, with a view to achieving a better understanding of the nature and role of trade unions in those countries. In his view, the report laid too much stress on the links between political parties and trade unions, something which clearly reflected unfamiliarity with the specific place and role of trade unions in the socialist countries. Forms of action could be very different, as was shown by the Yugoslav example.

47. Speaking in a more general way, Mr. Svenningsen raised the question of whether it would be possible to publish the various trade union studies in the national languages. Mr. Heldal asked for further information on this point. Mr. Bolin explained that any country concerned might obtain from the ILO a licence to translate and publish one of the trade union studies if it abided by the decisions taken by the Governing Body, in particular in the case of the two previous studies, to publish them together with the relevant discussions in the Working Party and in the Governing Body itself.

48. With regard to the studies on Spain and Yugoslavia, it was agreed that:
(a) the authors should be responsible for the final text of the studies and could make changes to correct factual inaccuracies;
(b) the two studies, accompanied by the report of the Working Party, should be submitted to the Governing Body at its 229th Session (February-March 1985);
(c) like the previous studies, they should be published, together with the discussion to which they had given rise.

49. It was also decided that the studies should remain confidential until the Working Party had approved its report.

Extract from the Minutes of the 229th Session of the Governing Body

B

(Wednesday, 27 February 1985, morning)

The sitting opened at 11.45 a.m., with Mr. Deshmukh in the Chair.

. . . .

FIFTEENTH ITEM ON THE AGENDA

Report of the Working Party on European Trade Union Studies

   The Chairman recalled that, in accordance with the decision taken by the Governing Body at its 228th Session (November 1984), Spain and Yugoslavia had been invited to be represented at the discussion of this item by one person each from government, employers' and workers' circles. Those representatives were therefore entitled to speak if they so wished.

   Mr. Heldal (Government, Norway), speaking as Chairman of the Working Party, presented the report. The studies on the trade union situation and industrial relations in European countries had been undertaken in response to resolutions adopted unanimously by the Second and Third European Regional Conferences in 1974 and 1979. The first two studies, dealing with Hungary and Norway, had been examined by a working party in November 1983 and by the Governing Body at its February-March 1984 Session. The two further studies on Spain and Yugoslavia had been submitted to the Working Party he had chaired and which had met during the Governing Body's November 1984 Session. The Governing Body was now invited by the Working Party to examine these studies and to authorise their publication.

   While it should be stressed that these studies could not in any way be regarded as a substitute for the ILO's regular supervisory procedures, they contained much valuable information and provided a good basis for a "wide exchange of views and experiences and for a frank and objective confrontation of ideas with a view to achieving better knowledge and understanding", as called for in the 1974 resolution.

   He expressed gratitude to the Governments of Spain and Yugoslavia for having invited the ILO to carry out those studies and for the help given to the ILO missions. He thanked his colleagues in the Working Party for their co-operation and commended the ILO officials concerned on the excellent quality of their work.

   Miss Hak (Employer, Netherlands), who had been a member of the Working Party, associated herself with Mr. Heldal's comments. The two studies were extremely interesting and deserved to be widely read outside the ILO. The Employers' group could support the point for decision in the Working Party's report and looked forward to receiving the study dealing with Austria.

Mrs. Molkova (Government, Czechoslovakia) agreed that both studies made a useful contribution to a better understanding of the conditions in which trade unions operated in various countries, as workers' rights had to be viewed in their overall economic and social context. The study on Yugoslavia, like the earlier one on Hungary, would help to dispel misconceptions about the role of trade unions in countries with centrally planned economies. It showed how trade unions in those countries played a leading role in standard setting and in decision-making at all levels, from the enterprise to central planning. It would be useful to back this study up by an ILO seminar on the role of trade unions in socialist countries, with the participation of representatives of different systems, as proposed by the socialist countries in the Governing Body last year.

Mr. Timmer (Worker, Hungary) also welcomed the studies as contributing to a better understanding of the circumstances in which trade unions operated. The study on Spain illustrated how changed social conditions had benefited workers and, despite the lack of unity in the trade union movement, had resulted in social progress. The study on Yugoslavia showed how, under a socialist system, trade unions enjoyed extensive rights and influenced political, economic and social decisions. He supported the previous speaker in calling for an ILO seminar on the role of trade unions in socialist countries.

Mr. Toš (Government, Yugoslavia) stressed the importance of the decision to carry out studies on trade unions and industrial relations in European countries, which not only promoted a deeper understanding of industrial relations in particular countries but also provided a basis for friendly discussions to resolve all outstanding issues. He thanked the Office for carrying out the study on Yugoslavia, which ably presented the main features of the Yugoslav constitutional system, particularly as regards the role of trade unions therein. It also pointed realistically to some problems and contradictions inherent in implementing a historically young system such as that of socialist self-management. This system established *sui generis* relations between trade unions and the State and gave workers a key role in the political system. Self-management powers were exercised through a number of assemblies from the communal up to the federal level, in which the trade unions participated on a basis of equality. At the federal level, no important government decisions were taken without first consulting the trade unions as well as the Economic Chamber of Yugoslavia. The relations between trade unions and government agencies were thus based on the constitutionally defined forms of self-management and political decision-making and any problems encountered were overcome by mutual discussion on equal terms. Some of these problems, which mainly concerned the need to improve the efficiency of the self-management system in order to stabilise the economy, had been openly discussed with the ILO mission and were accurately described in the study.

Lastly, he thanked the ILO officials who had devoted much time to discussions and visits in Yugoslavia, thus enabling them to study conditions on the spot and to present faithfully in their report the realities of the trade union situation in his country. He was convinced that it would contribute to a better understanding of Yugoslavia's position on ILO issues.

Mr. Lacasa Aso (Employer, Spain) said that the comments he had made on behalf of the Spanish Confederation of Employers at the Working Party's meeting in November 1984 were duly reflected in its report. He congratulated the Office on the excellent work done and supported the point for decision.

Mr. Montalvo Correa (Government, Spain) expressed his Government's satisfaction with the study on Spain. It showed the far-reaching changes that had taken place in industrial relations in his country since the last ILO study dating back to 1968. These changes not only affected the national legislation but had also generated a deep sense of responsibility on the part of the Government and the social partners, who were acting together in a spirit of solidarity to overcome the present economic crisis.

His Government was grateful to the ILO officials responsible for preparing a study of such high technical quality, reflecting the true state of affairs in Spain, and also to the Chairman and members of the Working Party which examined it. It was the Government's intention to have it published in Spanish so as to make it available to broad sectors of the international community with which his country maintained close links. In conclusion, he reaffirmed Spain's attachment to the standards and work of the ILO.

Mr. Svenningsen (Worker, Denmark) stated that the views of the Workers were accurately summarised in paragraph 7 of the report. While they contributed extremely useful information, such studies could not replace the ILO's supervisory machinery. The two Governments concerned should be encouraged to publish the studies in their own countries, together with the discussions in the Working Party and the Governing Body.

Mr. Santillan Cabeza (Worker, Spain) associated himself with the remarks made by the representative of the Spanish Government and the representative of Spanish Employers concerning the study on Spain, which clearly brought out the great changes that had taken place in industrial relations since the advent of democracy.

Mr. Franić (Worker, Yugoslavia) mentioned that he had been associated with the work of the ILO mission during its stay in Yugoslavia and had also taken part in the proceedings of the Working Party. He endorsed the views of all the preceding speakers who had stressed the importance of such studies in promoting better mutual understanding of the situation in different countries.

Mr. Brown (Worker, United States) supported the comments made by Mr. Svenningsen on behalf of the Workers' group, particularly to the effect that such studies could not in any way be regarded as a substitute for the ILO's basic supervisory machinery. As he had already remarked when the Governing Body examined the first two studies, there were considerable differences between the national situations covered by the two studies now before the Governing Body. The one on Spain gave an accurate picture of developments that had taken place in that country, especially in the trade union field, since the end of the Franco regime. While not implying any criticism of its authors, he felt that the study on Yugoslavia was necessarily based on the information placed at the disposal of the ILO mission during its stay there. In his view, it did not fully reflect the political and economic realities and the basic problems that arose in that country in terms of worker representation. He did not believe that under the system of socialist self-management workers had any real possibility to express themselves freely or to act independently of the ruling Communist Party, which as in other countries in Eastern Europe laid down basic policy. While interesting economic developments had taken place recently, he stressed, as he had already done with regard to the earlier study on Hungary, that the leading role of the Party prevented the workers from effectively controlling their own destinies.

Mr. Soubbotine (Worker, USSR) considered that the previous speaker's remarks were unwarranted and irrelevant to the item being discussed, namely the Report of the Working Party on European Trade Union Studies.

Mr. Toš (Government, Yugoslavia) said that the Yugoslav system was wholly based on the self-management principle and on socialist ownership of the means of production. While this complex system was not easy to explain, the ILO study had successfully described the main features of the system as well as certain problems that had arisen in its application. Mr. Brown's remarks contained unwarranted insinuations about the Yugoslav situation that had no relevance to the study or to the application of ILO Conventions ratified by Yugoslavia.

Mr. Szikinger (Government, Hungary) stated that, in view of certain comments during the debate which had also touched upon the ILO study on Hungary, he wished to reaffirm his Government's view that the study on Hungary gave an accurate picture of the situation in his country. There was accordingly no reason for questioning the objectivity of that study at this stage.

Mr. Oechslin (Employer, France; Employer Vice-Chairman) stressed once again that the Employers did not consider ILO activities of this kind to be a substitute for its supervisory machinery. While both of the country studies now before the Governing Body made extremely instructive reading, they did not imply any judgement on the position of those countries from the point of view of their obligations under ILO standards, and the Employers did not feel themselves bound in any way by the findings contained in those studies.

Mr. Franić (Worker representative, Yugoslavia) observed that the terms of reference of the ILO mission to Yugoslavia, which were to examine the trade union situation and industrial relations in the country, had been extremely clear and did not imply gathering evidence slanted towards any particular line of thinking. The mission had carried out its task very ably.

Mr. Ventejol (Government, France), while considering both studies to be of high quality, agreed with the previous speakers who had stressed that such studies should not affect the normal functioning of the ILO's supervisory procedures.

The Governing Body adopted the recommendation in paragraph 5 of the Office paper.[1]

Note

[1] "5. *The Governing Body is therefore invited to examine these studies and the report of the Working Party and to authorise their publication together with the relevant discussions*" (Geneva, ILO, doc. GB 229/15/07, 4 Feb. 1985; mimeographed).